TWAYNE'S WORLD AUTHORS SERIES
A Survey of the World's Literature

RUSSIA

Charles Moser, George Washington University
EDITOR

Alexander Kuprin

TWAS 481

Alexander Kuprin

ALEXANDER KUPRIN

By NICHOLAS LUKER

University of Nottingham, England

TWAYNE PUBLISHERS
A DIVISION OF G. K. HALL & CO., BOSTON

Library of Congress Cataloging in Publication Data

Luker, N   J   L
  Alexander Kuprin.

   (Twayne's world authors series ; TWAS : Russia)
   Bibliography: p.
   Includes index.
   1. Kuprin, Aleksandr Ivanovich, 1870–1938.
2. Authors, Russian — 20th century — Biography.
3. Journalists — Russia — Biography. I. Title.
PG3467.K8Z84   891.7'3'3 [B]   78–1535
ISBN 0–8057–6322–8

To the Memory of
my daughter, Taisya Clare,
who brought so much in so little time

Contents

About the Author

Nicholas Luker is a Yorkshireman by birth but spent part of his childhood in South Africa. After teaching himself Russian, he read French and Russian at Hertford College, Oxford, and in 1971 was awarded a PhD for a study of the life and works of Alexander Grin. He has produced critical work on Grin, compiled bibliographies on both Grin and Kuprin, and translated Grin, Kuprin and Bunin.

Dr. Luker has travelled widely in the Soviet Union, North America and southern Africa, and in 1976 was Visiting Lecturer in Russian at Victoria University of Wellington, New Zealand.

He is currently Lecturer in Russian at the University of Nottingham, England. He is married and has one son.

Preface

This book attempts what is well-nigh impossible. In some two hundred pages it surveys the life and work of Alexander Kuprin, whose writings in their most recent collected form run to well over four thousand pages. My task is the more difficult because there is no published study of Kuprin available in English. Therefore, this monograph aims to be as comprehensive as the limits of space stipulated for this series allow.

With Chekhov and Gorky, Kuprin was one of the best known Russian prose writers of the early 1900s. Time, however, has wrapped him in obscurity, and while his more famous contemporaries are well known in the West, Kuprin has received scant critical attention here. This study aims to redress the balance somewhat, by tracing the events of Kuprin's life and examining his writing, paying particular attention to *Moloch* (1896) and *The Duel* (1905), in Chapters 2 and 4 respectively. At the same time an effort has been made to examine Kuprin's work as a journalist, especially in his early years in Kiev, since this aspect of his career in particular suffers from critical neglect.

There is no complete edition of Kuprin's works. By far the best edition currently available is the recent nine-volume *Sobranie sochinenii* (Collected Works), published in Moscow from 1970 to 1973. It is to this edition that reference is made in the text of this study. Where more than one quotation is given from the same page, only the first carries a reference in the text. All translations from Kuprin's Russian are my own, as are those derived from Russian critical sources.

I wish to thank the many staff of Nottingham University Library for their kind assistance, and in particular Garth Terry and Glenis Pickering for their tireless help in obtaining research material from abroad. My thanks must also go to Dorothy Honniball, who typed my manuscript with such cheerful application and exemplary accuracy. To my wife Patricia I owe an inestimable debt of gratitude.

Preface

Without her constant encouragement and unremitting selflessness this study would never have been possible.

NICHOLAS LUKER

Nottingham, England

Chronology

1902   February: Marries Maria Karlovna Davydova (1881–1966), adopted daughter of editor of *God's World*. Leaves *Journal for All*. Visits Crimea. Meets Tolstoy in Yalta. Tales "The Swamp" and "At the Circus" published.
1903   Daughter Lidia born.
1904   Ceases editorial work for *God's World*. Begins intensive work on *The Duel*.
1905   May 3: *The Duel* published. Autumn: stays in Balaklava, Crimea; sees mutinous cruiser *Ochakov* shelled in Sevastopol. December: expelled from Balaklava for sketch "Events in Sevastopol."
1906   "The River of Life" and "Gambrinus" published. Travels widely: Crimea, Petersburg, Helsinki.
1907   March 31: divorced from first wife. December: moves to Gatchina near Petersburg.
1908   Publishes *Sulamith*. April 21: second daughter, Ksenia, born.
1909   September 17: marries Elizaveta Moritsevna Geinrikh (1882–1943). October: awarded Pushkin Prize jointly with Bunin. Third daughter, Zinaida, born. Dies in infancy.
1910   June 14: mother dies.
1911   Buys house in Gatchina. Tale "The Bracelet of Garnets" and Black Sea cycle *The Lestrigons* published.
1912   Visits southern Europe: Nice, Marseille, Venice, Genoa, Livorno, Corsica.
1913   Publishes "Anathema" and travel sketches, *Côte d'Azur*.
1914   August: opens military hospital in Gatchina house. Visits front. November: called up as lieutenant. Seven months' service in Finland.
1915   April: declared unfit for further military service. June: last part of novel *The Pit* published.
1916   Lecture tour of Caucasus. Falls ill with malaria.
1917   Late February: returns to Gatchina. From May edits Socialist Revolutionary paper *Free Russia* for two months.
1918   December 25: visits Lenin in Kremlin to discuss project for paper *Land* for peasantry.
1919   October: Gatchina taken by Whites. November: leaves Gatchina for Yamburg and Revel. December: leaves with family for Helsinki.
1920   January–July: works on paper *New Russian Life* in Helsinki. June: leaves by sea for Paris, arriving July 4.

Chronology

1921   Works on Paris Russian émigré journal *The Fatherland*.

1924   Daughter Lidia dies in Moscow.

1928   Novel *The Junkers* begins in serial form in paper *La Renaissance*. September: visits Belgrade for congress of Russian writers. Travel sketches *Yugoslavia* published.

1929   Publishes *Cape Huron* cycle about stay in Provence.

1931   Edits Paris weekly *Illustrated Russia* for year.

1933   Publishes tale *Jeannette*.

1934   Russian library opened in Kuprin's flat and run by his wife.

1937   May 29: leaves Paris by train for USSR; arrives Moscow May 31. In June moves to Golitsyno outside city, in December to Leningrad.

1938   Goes to Gatchina for summer, but becomes seriously ill. August 25: dies of cancer of oesophagus. August 27: buried in Leningrad.

CHAPTER 1

Biography and Literary Beginnings

I *Homme de valeur*

I T was Alexander Kuprin's good fortune to become a legend in
his own lifetime. A man of Herculean strength and irrepressible
vitality, he seemed to those who knew him in his prime a latter-day
bogatyr', one of the epic heroes of Russian folklore renowned for
their miraculous energy and resourcefulness. His squat, massive
frame with its mighty chest and sinewy neck told of exceptional
vigor and strength, expressed in his uncompromising face with its
narrow eyes. It was the supreme physicality of his tastes that distinguished Kuprin most sharply from his fellow writers. More often
than not, the refinement and sophistication of city *littérateurs*
brought out the aggressively defiant animal in him. "How much of
the wild beast there was about him," recalled the writer Ivan
Bunin, "—his sense of smell, for instance, which was remarkable
— and how much of the Tatar!"[1]

As an athlete Kuprin was superb. Had he not become a writer, he
could certainly have been a champion boxer or wrestler, sports in
which he excelled. Not satisfied with his prowess in these spheres,
he threw himself into a host of others — fencing, skating,
bicycling, horseriding, and even ballooning and aviation, the latter
two in particular helping to satisfy his craving for dangerous risks.
His indefatigable nature and love of physical excellence are perhaps
best summed up by the laconic epitaph he once jokingly asked to
have put on his gravestone: "Here lies a man who never wore
glasses."

As one who felt truly at home only amid the realities of life,
Kuprin flung himself into it with unparalleled zest. His appetite for

15

new experiences was voracious. Displaying an almost obsessive
desire to wrest as much from life as was humanly possible, he tried
dozens of occupations: soldier, reporter, stevedore, athlete, circus
rider, actor, dental technician, psalm reader, shop assistant,
forester, hunter, fisherman, bailiff, pig breeder, tobacco grower,
editor, and critic. It was even rumored that he once committed a
robbery so as to learn the feelings of a thief at work. Nor was this
the sum total of his experiences. Among his occupations were
others of a more bizarre kind: pupil in a choir school, student of art
and of Esperanto, novice monk, and lavatory pan salesman. Moreover, his gifts as a performer were outstanding. Not only was he a
skilled juggler; Anton Chekhov considered him so good an actor
that he urged him to join the Moscow Arts Theatre.

Kuprin's character was as complex as his experiences. Bunin
sums it up: "together with great pride there was unexpected
modesty, together with bad temper and insolence — great kindness
of heart, lack of malice, a shyness which was often almost pathetic,
naiveté, simple-heartedness . . . and a boyish gaiety. . ."[2] An eccentric of great personal charm, when angry Kuprin became a savage,
reckless animal. This was especially so when he was drunk: in a
rage he would tear off the tablecloth and send crockery and food
crashing to the floor.

No doubt the self-repression resulting from the restrictive years
spent in institutions in his youth does much to explain the
insatiability of Kuprin's physical life. The reaction came after he
left the army, when he could at last assert his ego with a vengeance.
Experience and diversity became his lifelong watchwords, a credo
expressed simply in a lecture he gave to journalists in Petrograd in
1918, when he advised them to "see everything, know everything,
do everything, and write about everything."[3] Several of his heroes
refer to their own driving, boundless curiosity. One of the most
autobiographical is Platonov of the novel *Yama* (*The Pit,* 1915),
who tells of the varied jobs he has had and adds: "Really and truly,
for a few days I'd like to become a horse, a plant, or a fish, or be a
woman and experience childbirth: I'd like to live the inner life of
everyone I meet and look at the world through their eyes" (VI,229).

Autobiographical elements abound in Kuprin's writing, based as
it so often is on events of his varied life. He was always reluctant to
use in his fiction characters or situations with which he was not
closely familiar, and he freely admitted the overwhelming importance of his own life for his work. In a letter of 1917 to the literary

historian S.A. Vengerov he wrote: "almost all my works are my autobiography. Sometimes I would invent an external plot, but the canvas on which I wove was all made of pieces of my own life."[4] Perhaps his myriad adventures the length and breadth of Russia did most to make Kuprin the very "unliterary" writer he was. Not fond of literary cliques with their petty rivalries, he spoke scornfully of urban literatı who spent their lives closeted in a study. He preferred to follow Chekhov's advice and "travel in a third class carriage," face to face with his fellow men. Always more at home among fishermen, laborers, and peasants, and more proud of his talents as a hunter or horticulturalist than of his success as an author, he felt that participation in the simple life of ordinary folk brought greater rewards than the monotonous and often lonely life of a writer at his desk. And yet, somehow, Kuprin managed to combine the two, so that his life, lived with the amazing versatility characteristic of him, became the very stuff of which his fiction was made.

II *Life*

The circumstances of Kuprin's early life were far from auspicious. Born in 1870 into a poor family in the remote South Russian town of Narovchat in Penza Province, he was left fatherless at the age of one. Until his death of cholera at thirty-seven, the boy's father, Ivan Ivanovich Kuprin, was a minor government official. Though his career was undistinguished, he displayed some artistic ability, being a fair violinist and painter in oils. Kuprin's mother, Lyubov Alekseevna, came from a once famous line of Tatar princes, the Kulunchakovs, whose impoverishment by the mid-1800s was so severe that she inherited only a small estate in the province. Throughout her life she remained passionately devoted to her youngest child and only son.[5] An intelligent, perceptive woman with an agile, progressive mind, she was fond of literature and took a keen interest in political events of the time. Kuprin always valued his mother's judgment about his work more than any other. Shortly before her death in 1910, he wrote: "I need you very much now. Not your experience or intelligence, but your instinctive taste, which I trust more than all today's criticism."[6] From his mother the boy inherited a profound sensitivity and vivid imagination, together with a fiery impulsiveness that he later called a facet of his "elemental Tatar nature." Kuprin was always inordinately proud of his Tatar stock: he boasted to friends of his descent from

Genghis Khan and Tamerlane, though in fact he had no such illustrious pedigree.

Some two years after Ivan Kuprin's death, the family moved to Moscow, where Lyubov Alekseevna obtained a place in the Widows' Home in Kudrino. Her son spent the next fifteen years in institutions in that city, living first with his mother in the home (a period reflected in his tale "Sviataia lozh" ["A White Lie," 1914]), then in the charitable Razumovsky boarding school, before entering the Second Moscow Military High School (*gimnazia*) in 1880. So unhappy were these early years that later he said sadly, "I had no childhood." The joylessness of this time finds frequent reflection in his work, notably in the gloomy recollections of his heroes in the tales "Reka zhizni" ("The River of Life," 1906), "Lenochka" (1910), and the strongly autobiographical "Na perelome" ("At the Turning Point," 1900), subtitled "Kadety" ("The Cadets"). In the latter Kuprin emphasizes what he loathed most about his schooling: the regular and accepted use of brute force, be it the vicious bullying of younger boys by their older fellows or the systematic beatings inflicted by the staff. Vividly he conveys the humiliation felt by his young hero Bulanin at being flogged for a trifling prank. "Bulanin is myself," he wrote barely a year before his death, "and the memory of the birching in the Cadet Corps remained with me for the rest of my life."[7]

In the autumn of 1888, Kuprin left the Cadet Corps to enter the Alexander Military Academy in Moscow, an institution that trained officers for infantry service in two years. Like the Cadet Corps, the Academy was a highly conservative establishment. The Junkers, as its inmates were known, were trained to consider themselves a privileged caste being groomed for high responsibility in the tsarist army.

In the summer of 1890, Kuprin graduated from the Academy with the rank of sublieutenant and was posted to the forty-sixth Dnieper Infantry Regiment stationed in the small Ukrainian town of Proskurov (now Khmelnitsky), west of Zhitomir in southwest Russia. Here and in the neighboring settlements of Gusyatin and Volochisk, near the Austrian border, he spent the next four years, the whole of his army service. Life for the young officer in this remote corner of the Russian empire was excruciatingly tedious, devoid of cultural pursuits and totally cut off from events in the world at large.

Upon leaving the army in 1894, Kuprin went to Kiev, where he engaged in journalistic work of many kinds. In September of 1901 he was invited by V.S. Mirolyubov, editor of the popular Petersburg monthly *Zhurnal dlia vsekh (Journal for All)*, to join his staff. In December Kuprin began work in the capital.

February of 1902 saw Kuprin's marriage to Maria Karlovna Davydova, the adopted daughter of Alexandra Davydova, widow of the director of the Petersburg Conservatoire. On her husband's death in 1889, Alexandra Davydova had become editor of the liberal Petersburg monthly *Mir bozhii (God's World)*. When she died early in 1902, Maria Karlovna took over *God's World,* and in February of that year Kuprin left the *Journal for All* to head the fiction section of his wife's journal.

Kuprin's activity after the publication of *Poedinok (The Duel)* in 1905 was not confined to the written word. He put himself forward as an elector to the first State Duma for the city of Petersburg, established links with sailors in the Black Sea Fleet in Sevastopol, and even attempted to enlist on the battleship *Potemkin,* which mutinied in June 1905. In official eyes he became politically unreliable, and was put under police surveillance.

The outbreak of the First World War saw Kuprin turning his energies to practical account once more. Only two weeks after the declaration of war he opened a military hospital in his Gatchina home, and then visited towns on the western front. Toward the end of 1914 he appealed through the press for money for the wounded, and in December rejected the idea of any celebrations to mark the twenty-fifth anniversary of his literary activity. As a reserve officer, he was called up in November 1914, and commanded an infantry company in Finland till May of 1915, when he was discharged on grounds of ill health. For the same reason he could not become a war correspondent, a post he had sought earlier during the Russo-Japanese War of 1904–1905.

On October 16, 1919, Gatchina was taken by White forces under General Nikolay Yudenich. For a fortnight Kuprin was obliged to edit *Prinevskii krai (Neva Country),* a paper published by Yudenich's army headquarters. When in October the Whites retreated westward before the Red Army, Kuprin traveled with them to Yamburg (now Kingisepp), where he joined his wife and daughter. Via Narva, the family reached Revel (now Tallin) in Estonia, and in December left for Finland. After six months in Helsinki, where Kuprin worked on the émigré paper *Novaia russkaia zhizn' (New Russian Life),* they sailed for France, arriving in Paris in early July of 1920.

There followed long years of poverty and debt. The income from what writing Kuprin did was extremely small, and his wife's brave attempts to establish a book-binding shop and an émigré library were financial disasters. A return to the Soviet Union offered the only solution to Kuprin's material and psychological difficulties, but it was late 1936 before he made the decision to apply for a visa. Anticipating censure from other émigrés, Kuprin and his wife prepared to leave very quickly, keeping their departure secret. On May 29, 1937, seen off only by their daughter, they left the Gare du Nord for Moscow.

When on May 31 the Kuprins arrived in Moscow, they were met by representatives of writers' organizations and installed in the Metropole Hotel. In early June they moved to a dacha owned by the Union of Writers at Golitsyno, outside Moscow, where Kuprin received medical attention and rested till the winter. In mid-December he and his wife moved to an apartment in Leningrad.

By early 1938 Kuprin's health was failing rapidly. Though later weeks brought a temporary improvement that encouraged the couple to go to Gatchina for the summer, his condition was clearly hopeless. Already suffering from a kidney disorder and sclerosis, he had now developed cancer of the oesophagus. Surgery did little to help. He died on August 25, 1938, and was buried in the Volkov cemetery in Leningrad two days later.

III   *Early Verse*

Kuprin was ten when, in August 1880, he passed the entrance examination for the Military High School, renamed the Cadet Corps in 1882. In the stifling atmosphere of this military institution, the boy first took a serious interest in literature. Credit for this was largely due to M.I. Tsukhanov, a teacher of Russian literature (in *"The Cadets"* he appears as Trukhanov). To him Kuprin owed his lifelong love of Russian literature, and in particular of Pushkin.

Fired with enthusiasm by Tsukhanov's teaching, the boy began to write, turning to poetry as the best means of expressing his youthful aspirations. Kuprin was to write poems, epigrams, and aphorisms for the rest of his life, but in his adult years he was always most reluctant to publish them, feeling they were far inferior to his prose. Though he had written his first verse at the age of seven, most of his youthful poems — some thirty in all — date from the four years from 1883 to 1887, when he was in the Cadet Corps.[8]

The earliest of them, "Na den' koronatsii" ("On Coronation Day"), written in early 1883, was inspired by the celebrations for the crowning of Alexander III in May of that year. With youthful exuberance and naive delight, Kuprin portrays the jubilation of Muscovites at the festivities, stresses the sanctity of the tsar's person, and expresses the hope that God will preserve the new monarch from harm. Later poems demonstrate in fulsome terms the young man's love for his native land. Such, for example, is "Boets" ("The Warrior") of 1885, a heroic monologue uttered by a soldier dying on the battlefield. His last words summon his fellow warriors to continue the unequal struggle:

> Brothers! I perish . . . Take then the banner,
> And fearlessly face the foe.
> The people shed tears for you, brothers,
> Bitter tears and blood.[9]

More important are several satirical pieces, of which the best is his "Oda Katkovu" ("Ode to Katkov") of 1886. The poem ridicules the notorious obscurantist Mikhail Katkov on his appointment as minister of internal affairs by Alexander III. Using archaisms to comic effect, Kuprin writes with detestation of this arch-reactionary, who spoke haughtily of the Russian people as "peasants and wild animals" and dealt out harsh punishment to troublesome student leaders.

Perhaps the most interesting of Kuprin's early poems is the political piece "Sny" ("Dreams"), written on April 14, 1887, the day before sentence was passed on the terrorists who had plotted to assassinate Alexander III in March of that year. Among those subsequently condemned to death was Alexander Ulyanov, Lenin's brother. That the death sentence would be passed was never in doubt, and Kuprin's vivid imagination produced a lurid picture of the public hanging as he foresaw it: a noisy square filled with an angry crowd; the high, black gallows; the executioner awaiting his victims; and the horrific death throes of the condemned. The poem closes with words of bitter reproach at the tsar's "justice": "A vile, terrible deed is done."[10] Despite its artistic imperfections, of all Kuprin's early verse "Dreams" displays the greatest measure of sincere, though unsophisticated, political commitment.

Not all Kuprin's early verse was patriotic or political. Several poems — for instance "Pesn' skorbi" ("The Song of Sorrow"), "Grezy" ("Day Dreams"), and "Slezy besplodnye..." ("Futile tears...") of 1887 — speak of melancholy, hopelessness, and disillusionment, common motifs in the pessimistic poetry of the late 1800s. Other poems are love lyrics addressed to the objects of Kuprin's adolescent affections. Among them are "Zaria" ("Dawn"), "Vesna" ("Spring"), and the lyrical "Milye ochi, lazurnye ochi..." ("Dear eyes, azure eyes...") of 1887, dedicated to a distant relative of his from Penza. Apart from several poems devoted to revelry and the joys of youthful comradeship such as "Molitva p'iannitsy" ("A Drunkard's Prayer," 1884) and "Proiskhozhdenie kon'iaka" ("The Origin of Brandy," 1885), Kuprin wrote several humorous verses of an indecent kind, like "Masha," to which he later added the *caveat:* "Not to be read to anyone."

Though many poems by the young Kuprin are lacking in artistic merit, they do provide evidence of his growing literary awareness. They contain a surprising range of themes and styles, from the overtly political through the intimately lyrical to the scabrously erotic, a variety that foreshadows the wide spectrum of treatments seen in his prose. What is perhaps most significant about poems like "Ode to Katkov" and "Dreams" is that they reveal in the adolescent a high degree of social conviction, which however formless it was at this early stage, would receive more effective elaboration in such later prose works as *Molokh (Moloch,* 1896) and *The Duel* (1905).

IV *The First Tale*

It was in the Military Academy that Kuprin's writing career began. In 1889 he met Liodor Ivanovich Palmin, a well-known poet of the time who arranged for the publication of Kuprin's first tale, "Poslednii debiut" ("The Last Debut") in the Moscow weekly *Russkii satiricheskii listok (The Russian Satirical Leaflet)* for December 3, 1889. When Kuprin's authorship came to light (the tale was signed "A. K—rin") he was put under two days' arrest in the guardroom, as Junkers were forbidden to publish without the consent of the Academy authorities. Events surrounding the publication of this first work left a permanent mark on Kuprin. He first recalls the episode in his tale "Pervenets" ("The Firstling," 1897), altering the name of the journal and rechristening his mentor Ivan Liodorych Venkov. In the later autobiographical work *Iunkera* (*The Junkers,* 1928–1932), the affair is treated in more detail, while in the short tale "Tipograficheskaia kraska" ("Printer's Ink," 1929) he returns to the event yet again, this time with undisguised nostalgia.

As the basis of "The Last Debut," Kuprin took a real incident — the suicide by poisoning on stage of the singer E. P. Kadmina in 1881, a tragedy which also inspired Ivan Turgenev's tale "Clara Milich" and Chekhov's one act drama *Tatyana Repina.* The work tells of the tragic love of the actress Golskaya for the impresario Alexander Petrovich. Drama is both the setting and the substance of the tale. In Golskaya's dressing room between acts three and four, Petrovich breaks with her, urging her to forget all that has occurred between them and promising to provide for the child she is expecting. He then rebukes her for her poor performance in the play so far. Desperate at the loss of the man she loves, yet stung by his criticism of her acting ability, Golskaya goes out on stage, obliged "to entertain an audience of thousands just when she is perhaps close to suicide or madness" (I, 44). By a neat irony, her role on stage is that of a deceived girl, while the impresario plays her seducer. Thus their professional and private roles coincide and interlock. In the final act, playing out her inner pain, Golskaya performs with superb power. Of all those present, only her stage partner fails to understand her, for he cannot discern the woman through the actress.

Kuprin's first tale, with its unfelicitous title, has several defects that he later acknowledged. In particular, the sharp contrast between hero and heroine is a time-honored romantic cliché: he the cynical seducer, she the pure beauty destroyed by her selfless love for him. The contrast is made more blatant by the hackneyed description of their faces. His is typically demonic — "framed by a thick mane of black hair ... it bore the stamp of proud, self-assured strength" (I, 42) — and hers has earned her the name of goddess for its "classical profile and marblelike, translucently dull pallor" (I, 43). The convention is reinforced by the excessively pompous style used by both narrator and characters. Of Golskaya Kuprin writes: "Wringing her hands, she sobbed, she implored him for love, for mercy. She summoned him before the judgment of God and men, and wept once more, madly, desperately..." (I, 46). Moreover, the tale's plot is unashamedly melodramatic. Not content with his excessively sentimental portrayal of Golskaya in her hour of crisis, Kuprin has her take poison in full view of the audience as the curtain falls.

Despite its stilted language and stereotyped characters, "The Last Debut" has the narrative dynamism typical of the later Kuprin. At the same time, though beset by literary clichés, its treatment of love and the pain it can bring is deeply sensitive, a quality that would be the hallmark of his best works.

V *Regimental Service*

Kuprin's few years of military service saw the publication of several tales, among them "Psikheia" ("Psyche," 1892), "Lunnoi noch'iu" ("On a Moonlit Night"), "V pot'makh" ("In the Dark," 1893) and "Doznanie" ("The Enquiry," 1894). Only the last is concerned with the army; its predecessors are studies of mysterious or abnormal states of mind. With them belong other tales like "Slavianskaia dusha" ("A Slav Soul"), "Bezumie" ("Madness") and "Zabytyi potselui" ("The Forgotten Kiss"), all published in 1894, works in which Kuprin described himself as "a collector of rare and strange manifestations of the human soul."[11]

Some three years passed between the appearance of "The Last Debut" and the publication of his second tale, "Psyche," in December of 1892. Like "On a Moonlit Night" which followed it, it shows the aberrations of a deranged mind and investigates the blurred line between fantasy and reality. Subtitled "The Diary of a Sculptor," it describes a recluse who fashions from clay a statue of Psyche he has seen in a dream. His sensuality is so aroused by the beauty of his own making that he becomes convinced that by sheer willpower he can bring his statue to life. Imagining he sees his Psyche breathing, he kisses her and faints. Driven insane by the perverse creativity of his own mind, he is taken off to an asylum.

The diary form of the work, with its dates which drift from actuality into nonsense, and the imperceptible blending of reality and fantasy show similarities with Gogol's story "The Diary of a Madman." But Kuprin's focus on his hero's sick mind, with its extravagant phantasmagoria and fevered sexual fantasies, stems from the Decadent trends of the late 1800s.

"On a Moonlit Night" is similar in theme and mood. Probing the innermost recesses of the mind, Kuprin explores in his protagonist Gamov the Dostoevskian duality fundamental to the human soul. "You see," Gamov explains to the narrator, "I think there are two wills inherent in man. One is conscious . . . and I am constantly aware of its presence. . . . But the other is unconscious; on some occasions it controls a person completely without his knowledge, sometimes even against his will" (I, 140). When this second will is in chaos, Gamov explains, otherwise unthinkable acts of violence occur, like the brutal murder of his beloved, to which he tacitly confesses. Inflamed with passion for a beautiful girl who is openly scornful of him, he puts a revolver to her temple and demands that she surrender to him. The "unaccountable voluptuousness" (I, 143) he discovers in the situation is disrupted by her mocking laughter as she refuses to submit. Only when he has pulled the trigger does Gamov realize the full horror of what he has done.

The duality of the soul revealed in this "psychological étude," as Kuprin called it,[12] is pivotal to his more important work of that same year, "In the Dark," published in the journal *Russkoe bogatstvo (Russian Wealth)*. Some five times longer than "Psyche" and divided into fourteen chapters, it was his most ambitious tale so far, and indeed was subtitled *povest'*, or novelette. Traveling by night train to the provincial town of R. to take up her first appointment as governess, the heroine, Zinaida Pavlovna, is rescued from the attentions of a fellow passenger by a young engineer, Alexander Alarin. Once she is in R., Zinaida's employer, the rich industrialist Kashperov, becomes infatuated with her and determines to possess her. But only when Alarin faces imprisonment after gambling away official funds does Zinaida offer herself to Kashperov for money, so as to repay Alarin's debt. Admiring her selflessness, Kashperov gives her the money without any conditions. However, on seeing Alarin's base greed when she gives him the money, Zinaida is filled with contempt for him. She leaves him, falls ill from nervous shock, and dies. Kashperov kills himself by drinking prussic acid, and Alarin leaves the town a broken man, aged and prematurely grey.

On his own admission, Alarin is a "split personality" (I, 53). Described as "a representative of today's moral vacillation,"[13] he is an astonishing amalgam of contradictory traits. Though noble and sensitive, he can also be base and heartless; his energy and decision sometimes yield to weakness and apathy. As the story develops, Kuprin takes pains to show how different Alarin is from Zinaida, however alike they may seem at the outset: his noisy egocentricity and capricious changes of mood[14] are worlds away from her soft

sincerity and quietly heroic determination. When Zinaida brings
him the money, the negative side of Alarin's dual nature is revealed
in all its repulsiveness, that "dark, terrible side" deep in each of us
of which Gamov spoke (I, 139). The same "dark side" emerges in
Kashperov, too, when his lust for Zinaida reaches fever pitch:
"No. . . . I'll overcome you," he says, "I'll force you! You may be
pure, but I'll awaken such instincts in you that you won't know
yourself!' " (I, 75). Such fits of somber fury are another manifestation of the demonism already glimpsed in Petrovich of "The Last
Debut."

As if mirroring the duality revealed in his characters as the tale
progresses, Kuprin's narrative technique oscillates between opposite poles. He is deliberately plain and realistic in describing settings: the opening scene where Alarin's friends see him off from a
Moscow station (as Anatoly Volkov notes,[15] an episode stamped
with terse Chekhovian irony), the drab life of the town of R., and
early scenes in the Kashperov household. But when the tale is
highly charged with emotion — during Kashperov's assaults on
Zinaida's honor, and the final meeting between hero and heroine —
Kuprin creates an atmosphere of tragic gloom where fateful pas-
sions bind his characters inextricably together. The story's title is a
verbal distillation of the circumstances in which the characters find
themselves, a life of figurative darkness intensified by the physical
twilight that pervades the work.

While Kuprin's first large prose work shares many flaws of "The
Last Debut" — melodramatic passages, unnatural situations, and
bombastic language — it demonstrates his ability to handle success-
fully a complex plot with its major and minor characters, varied
settings, and dialogues.

"The Enquiry" was Kuprin's first army story and the most
important work of his years as a soldier. It was also the first in a
long series of tales about the military that culminated ten years later
in *The Duel*. The work was his first publication to arouse critical
comment. A critic for a Kiev newspaper grudgingly acknowledged
glimpses of talent in the tale, but chastised Kuprin for excessive
attention to detail and lack of spontaneous feeling.[16] For censorship reasons the manuscript title of the work "Ekzekutsiia" ("Corporal Punishment"), was changed to the less emotive "Iz otdalen-
nogo proshlogo" ("From the Distant Past") at the suggestion of
N. K. Mikhailovsky, editor of *Russian Wealth* where the tale
appeared in August of 1894, soon after Kuprin had left the army.

Its final title was chosen in the early 1900s. Apart from his growing dissatisfaction with army life, the imminent publication of "The Enquiry" was probably a major reason for Kuprin's resignation in the summer of 1894. There can be no doubt that the appearance of such a work, written by an officer and signed with his full name, would have had unpleasant consequences for him.

Set in a provincial garrison, the story tells how Kozlovsky, a young lieutenant in his first year of service, is ordered to conduct an enquiry into the theft of a pair of boot tops and thirty-seven kopecks by the Tatar Baiguzin. By appealing to the Tatar's filial feelings, Kozlovsky extracts a confession from him, and as a result Baiguzin is sentenced to a hundred strokes of the birch. As Kuprin revealed many years later in the tale "Rodina" ("Native Land"), the story is based on his own experience as an officer obliged to conduct such investigations.[17]

Despite the distancing device of the title suggested by Mikhailovsky, "The Enquiry" is a direct indictment of conditions in the Russian army in the 1890s. His involvement with Baiguzin shows Kozlovsky the absurdity of a system that punishes a man so harshly for so trivial an offense. Cruelly indifferent, that system takes no account of the man, here a Tatar, chosen by Kuprin to represent minority nationalities in the tsarist army. Bewildered in an alien environment where his natural instinct is simply to flee, Baiguzin is mocked and persecuted as an oddity. Kozlovsky realizes that to punish him in the prescribed way is senseless. The Tatar not only cannot see why his deed is wrong, but also can barely understand Russian. Far from correcting him, a flogging will only embitter him.

"The Enquiry" is central to Kuprin's development because in Kozlovsky it presents the first in a succession of sensitive young officers at odds with their fellows and painfully aware of the injustice prevalent in the army. That type is continued in figures like Yakhontov of "Pokhod ("The March," 1901), and exemplified by Romashov of *The Duel*. Impressionable and humane, Kozlovsky is horrified by the flogging of Baiguzin and appalled at his fellow officers' indifference to what he considers a travesty of justice. Because of his role in the investigation, he feels responsible for the punishment inflicted on the Tatar, and as an officer he feels guilty at being part of the army hierarchy that condones such excessive violence. Paradoxically, it is their officially distanced positions as accuser and accused that bring officer and soldier spiritually to-

gether. At the Tatar's mention of his mother far away, Kozlovsky
sadly recalls his own mother a thousand versts away and realizes
that without her he too is utterly alone in this isolated corner of
Russia. His recollection forges a tenuous link: "Between the second
lieutenant and the silent Tatar there suddenly sprang up a delicate,
tender bond" (I, 152). After the flogging, as both suffer in their
different ways, their eyes meet across the barrack square — "and
again the lieutenant felt between himself and the soldier a strange,
spiritual bond" (I, 157).

Yet despite his sympathy for Baiguzin and his noble intentions to
have the sentence reduced, Kozlovsky fails to help him. Inexpe-
rienced in the company of his fellow officers, he lacks the confidence that might have enabled him to alleviate the Tatar's lot.
Moreover, his inner weakness leaves the conflict between his duty
as an officer and his sympathy as a man unresolved. Allowing himself to be deflected from his purpose by the company commander,
to whom he turns for advice, Kozlovsky falls victim to the same
indifferent system that sentences Baiguzin to the rod. But he is
executioner too, for he feels he has tricked the soldier into confess-
ing his crime. For all its impassioned sincerity, his angry retort at
the close of the tale to a sadistic fellow officer who declares the
flogging insufficiently severe ends only in hysterics: "... suddenly
covering his face with his hands, he burst into loud sobs, shudder-
ing with his whole body like a weeping woman and feeling painfully, cruelly ashamed of his tears..." (I, 158).

In many ways "The Enquiry" is a preliminary sketch for *The
Duel* a decade later. Pointers to Kuprin's novel are also to be found
in his other army work of 1894, the humorous tale "Kust sireny"
("The Lilac Bush"), whose obtuse officer-protagonist Almazov
and his ambitious wife Verochka clearly foreshadow Nikolaev and
Shurochka in *The Duel*.

Kuprin's resignation from the army in 1894 was a watershed in
his life. The next seven years, till his departure for Petersburg in
1901, were to be a period of immensely rich experience and creativity. They would encompass not only kaleidoscopic journalistic
work, many temporary jobs, and extensive travel, but also the publication of two collections of his works and, among others, the tale
Moloch, which first brought him fame.

CHAPTER 2

Kiev Years

I *Kiev Papers and* Kiev Types

K UPRIN arrived in Kiev without friends or acquaintances, and with only four roubles in his pocket. Even worse, he realized with dismay he had no knowledge that would equip him for civilian life. It was now that the narrowness of military training made itself felt: "I realized ... no talent is worth a thing without systematic education."[1] His own lack of systematic education was to dog him all his life, and he believed it the greatest disadvantage a writer could suffer.

A "free bird" in a city full of promise, Kuprin had set his heart on a literary career. By September 1894, he had begun work on the papers *Kievskoe slovo (Kiev Word)* and *Zhizn' i iskusstvo (Life and Art),* and the following February he joined *Kievlianin (The Kievan),* the first two papers being liberal in their sympathies and the latter monarchist. Kuprin's choice of these and other papers during his years as a journalist hardly ever reflected his political views. Never very definite in his political attitudes anyway, in Kiev he was often penniless, and had to turn his hand to whatever newspaper work presented itself.

This is not to say that Kuprin regarded his years as a journalist as a time of drudgery, or a reporter's work as insignificant. Acknowledging later the incalculable experience he had gained from his Kiev years, he maintained that journalism was the finest apprenticeship for a writer. He had especially high regard for the work of reporters in the field, the "newspaper infantry," as he called them: "The reporter weaves the pattern of life ... this pattern is precious, and that is why a reporter's work is precious too."

The qualities necessary in a good journalist, he believed, were "mad courage, audacity, breadth of view, and an amazing memory,"[2] gifts he himself possessed in full measure. Kuprin's work as a reporter was very varied; he wrote leading articles, reviews, anecdotes, sketches, short stories, poems, and accounts of city events, court proceedings, and theater and circus performances. Paid in his first months only two kopecks a line, he was often compelled to be less than honest, for example contributing pieces on European events and signing himself the paper's "foreign correspondent." He wrote an enormous number of articles, the majority of them difficult to trace since they bear no signature. Especially interesting are those showing his concern with agrarian problems, such as the difficulties of land shortage, the resettlement of peasants, and the drainage of marshland. Nor were the Kiev papers the only ones to which he contributed. On his frequent journeys to southwest Russia he wrote for papers in provincial towns he visited — Zhitomir, Novocherkassk, Rostov-on-Don, and Odessa. Few works of this time bore his full signature. If he signed them at all, he used either a pseudonym or cryptonym.[3]

Among his more important contributions to the Kiev papers were Kuprin's accounts of contemporary city life. He wrote a Sunday *feuilleton* for *Life and Art* entitled "Kaleidoscope" and signed "Zarathustra," a weekly chronicle of Kievan events, full of topical issues and often humorously critical of the city authorities. Many features of the *feuilleton* appear in the unfinished satirical comedy *Gran' stoletiia (The Edge of the Century),* written by Kuprin and a journalist friend.[4] Similar to "Kaleidoscope" was his series of "Malen'kie khroniki" ("Little Chronicles"), which appeared in *The Kiev Word* throughout 1895. Topicality is the keynote of these frequently satirical miniatures of Kiev life, which touch on everything from the plight of the city's poor and the inadequacies of the local opera to the inefficiency of urban administration and the risks to health from unheated railway carriages. Particularly interesting is "Zagadochnyi smekh" ("Mysterious Laughter"), in which Kuprin shows his anger at the audience during a performance of Tolstoy's drama *The Power of Darkness* in December of 1895. Many members of the audience, he writes, laughed aloud during the most tragic scenes, a reaction he sees as proof of the indifference of Kievans to true dramatic art.[5]

More significant than either his *feuilletons* or chronicles were Kuprin's sketches (*ocherki*), his favorite genre during his Kiev years. The distinction between sketch and tale (*rasskaz*) is difficult to draw; Gorky attempted to solve the problem by describing the *ocherk* as "somewhere between investigation (*issledovanie*) and story."[6] To this one might add that Kuprin's sketches are investigations of particular environments, such as a factory or mine, or portraits of people typical of specific social classes, occupations, or circumstances. Description and documentation are paramount, and there is no hint of a story line. Sketches were written by many nineteenth century Russian writers, notably Vladimir Korolenko and Gleb Uspensky. Moreover, the genre was familiar to readers of both metropolitan and provincial newspapers in the 1890s.[7]

Kuprin's contributions to the genre fall into two distinct groups. The first consists of four industrial sketches that serve as preliminary drafts for the setting of *Moloch*. The second group — collectively entitled *Kievskie tipy (Kiev Types)* — are sixteen in number, and are descriptive portraits of types of people observed by Kuprin in the city. Almost all appeared in one of two papers, *The Kiev Word* and *Volyn' (Volhynia),* eleven between October and December of 1895, the remaining five between 1896 and 1898. March of 1896 saw the publication of eight of the sketches in a small edition entitled *Kiev Types,* Kuprin's first book.

In his foreword to the collection Kuprin wrote that his intention was to portray "the collective traits of those groups of individuals on whom certain occupations and local conditions have had one effect or another." To stress the fact that his characters were representative types rather than specific individuals, he added: "I . . . warn the reader that in the sketches offered he will not find a single photograph, despite the fact that every trait is carefully drawn from life."[8] For all his assertions that his *Types* are based on actual people, Kuprin injects more of his creative self into them than he does into his documentary industrial sketches, and that brings his Kiev pieces closer to the *rasskaz* genre proper.

Kiev Types presents an entire gallery of people though with emphasis on people of the lower classes whom Kuprin came to know through his work as a reporter. He identifies his characters, not by name, but by the social or occupational group to which they belong: Dnieper Sailor, False Witness, Chorister, Fireman, Landlady, Down-and-Out, Thief, Doctor, Religious Hypocrite, and Dealer in Dirty Pictures.

The first to appear was the highly successful "Student-Dragun" ("The Student-Dragoon," 1895), a satirical portrait of the rich young men studying in Kiev. In brief but withering strokes Kuprin sketches the type. Devoid of initiative and thoroughly debauched, the student is a mental and spiritual cripple, indifferent to art, science, and social issues. He is good at billiards, frequently in debt, shows off in fashionable restaurants, and avoids his mother on the street because he is ashamed of her. In order to acquire a smart pair of trotters and a permanently bulging wallet, he is even prepared to play gigolo to some aging woman who refuses to submit to the ravages of time.

"Doktor" ("The Doctor"), of the same year, describes the gradual erosion of a young physician's idealism as he grows richer and older. Perceptively and humorously, Kuprin divides Kiev doctors into four broad types: the cheerful, the pessimistic, the women's doctor, and the "speculator." He employs the same technique of classification of types within a type in several other sketches. "Lzhesvidetel' " ("The False Witness") divides that type into three: those used by notaries and by advocates, and those used in divorce cases. "Pevchii" ("The Chorister") distinguishes four kinds of singer in Kiev's churches: the novice descant, the experienced descant, the tenor, and the bass; while "Khanzhushka" ("The Religious Hypocrite") manifests herself in two forms, the faster and the gourmande.

Several sketches — like "Bosiak" ("The Down-and-Out") and "Vor" ("The Thief") — explore the twilight world of back street Kiev, with its taverns and cheap lodgings, its beggars and whores. "The Thief" reveals Kuprin's astonishingly detailed knowledge of the city's multifarious pickpockets and petty criminals, as he describes their training, specializations, and techniques. Linguistically, the sketch is highly original, brimming with thieves' jargon and spiced with local ditties.

One of the most interesting items in the collection is the satirical sketch "Khudozhnik" ("The Artist," 1896), which displays Kuprin's scorn for Decadent art of the time. Landscape painters to a man and mediocre at best, Kiev artists of this category proclaim themselves innovators and reject all art of the past, from Michelangelo to Van Dyck. "We are Impressionists!" they cry, and for this reason, Kuprin explains mockingly, they paint "the snow violet, a dog pink, beehives in the apiary . . . lilac, and the sky green. . ." (I, 411).

In *Types* Kuprin focuses primarily on the intriguing, an emphasis not essentially different from that of works like "Psyche" and "On a Moonlit Night.'' Still, however revealing his treatment, it is broad rather than deep, and involves no exploration of individual psychology. Nevertheless, valuable in the documentary sense as firsthand pictures of figures central to Kiev life, the sketches are remarkable for their color, clarity, and scrupulous attention to detail. Moreover, they claimed a place in Kuprin's mental treasure house of vivid impressions. Thus several *Types* served as preliminary sketches for later fictional works: the landlady of "Kvartirnaia khoziaika" reappears in Anna Fridrichovna of "The River of Life"; elements of "The Student-Dragoon" emerge in Sobashnikov of *The Pit;* and features of "The Down-and-Out" and "The Thief" find their way into such tales as "S ulitsy" ("Off the Street," 1904), and "Obida" ("An Insult," 1906).

II Miniatures

October of 1897 saw the appearance in Kiev of Kuprin's second collection, *Miniatiury (Miniatures),* twenty-five short stories published in Kiev papers over the previous three years.

Thematically very varied, the tales are of uneven quality and devoid of unifying ideas. Several of them resemble earlier works like "Psyche" in their exploration of exceptional states of mind. "A Slav Soul" tells of Yas, a faithful servant who hangs himself after seeing a suicide. The reason for this, the narrator concludes, lay in his "strange soul . . . loyal, pure, contradictory, cantankerous, and sick . . . a real Slav soul" (I, 167). "Natalya Davydovna" develops the psychopathic sexual element already glimpsed in "Psyche." The heroine of the title leads a double life: a respected teacher in a school for daughters of the nobility, once every two or three months she becomes a nymphomaniac, picking up men on the street and taking them to a cheap hotel on the outskirts of town. After a night of monstrous debauchery she returns demurely to school. When a soldier dies in her arms and she is exposed, she tells the investigator of the incomparable pleasure she has derived from playing the roles of prim paragon by day and insatiable Messalina by night. The same contrast between appearance and reality occurs in other tales in which sex plays a part, such as "Strashnaia minuta" ("A Terrible Moment"), "Skazka" ("A Fairy Tale"), and "Bez zaglaviia" ("Without a Title"). "A Terrible Moment" is remarkable for its subtle analysis of the feelings of an attractive young woman torn between her desire for sexual experience with an irresistible stranger and her duty as a mother and wife. None of these tales, however, even remotely approaches the pathological sexual excess of "Natalya Davydovna."

Linked with them are other tales such as "Strannyi sluchai" ("A Strange Occurrence"), the melodramatic "Kapriz" ("Caprice"), and the Eastern legend "Al'-Issa," which tell of the inconstancy of women and the suffering they inflict on those who love them. While the cynical widow of "A Strange Occurrence" drives a young writer to suicide by mocking his love for her, the chivalrous hero of "Al'-Issa" finds himself committed to love not the beautiful goddess whom he has sought, but a toothless hag.

Other *Miniatures* reveal Kuprin's sympathetic interest in people of specific occupations. Such are the circus tales "Lolli" and "Allez!" and the analogous story of lions "V zverintse" ("At the Menagerie"), all of which exhibit his close knowledge of circus life. One of his best known circus stories, "Allez!" lays bare the hypocrisy of circus life and the cruel amorality behind its tinsel façade. Neat, economical, and skillfully built round its triggering leitmotif of the circus command "allez!", the work earned high praise from Tolstoy.[9] One of Kuprin's most successful circus tales, it belongs with such other works as "V tsirke" ("At the Circus," 1902), and the one act play *Kloun (The Clown)* of 1897, staged in St. Petersburg in 1907.

The moving autobiographical tale "Kliacha" ("The Jade") investigates an occupation with which Kuprin was even more familiar, that of the provincial journalist. Its hero, Pashkevich, is a literary thoroughbred forced to become a hack to survive. "He had to live," the narrator explains, "nobody would have given him his dinner ... just because of his talent" (II, 52). Grinding poverty and the grueling labor of a provincial reporter destroy both his literary gift and his health. Stricken with blindness and consumption, he dies in four years, the victim of social and economic circumstance.

Surprisingly, only a handful of *Miniatures* continue the portrayal of army life begun in "The Enquiry." "Nochleg" ("A Night's Lodging") conveys the fatigue of soldiers tramping the Russian countryside, but shows their martial pride when they are billeted in a village for the night. Its plot, like that of the anecdotal "Breget" ("Bréguet"), relies heavily on coincidence. Hearing a woman's voice in the house where he is quartered, Lieutenant Avilov recognizes it as that of a girl he raped six years before in Tula Province.

"Marianna," a tale within a tale like several of the miniatures, is a light, humorous piece resembling love stories of Maupassant or Turgenev. Its narrator reminisces with regret about his youth in the army, when he missed an opportunity for an affair with the regimental commander's wife because he was too hesitant in his advances.

Perhaps the most interesting tale in the collection is the allegorical "Sobach'e schast'e" ("Dogs' Happiness"), in which Kuprin uses a "conversation" between stray dogs in a cage en route to the pound to illustrate the inequality and oppression prevalent in Russia. The inmates of the cage are a canine cross-section in breed and attitude, from the "aristocratic" old Dane, through the "liberally inclined" poodle, down to the "violet mongrel" lying sullenly in a corner. The animals agree with the eloquent poodle that men are evil creatures, greedier than any dog in the world: "one tenth of them have seized all the vital supplies for themselves . . . and make the other nine-tenths starve." Referring to such things as prison and censorship, the poodle asks: "Would one dog . . . forbid another to breathe the fresh air and express his thoughts freely on the organization of dogs' happiness?" Moreover, he adds, though dogs sometimes bite, unlike men they never destroy one another out of love, envy, or spite. Though he concludes that men are "hypocritical, envious, deceitful, inhospitable, and cruel" (I, 47), the poodle declares that the situation cannot be corrected, because man is in command and always will be. It is impossible for dogs to be free, for a dog's life is firmly in man's hands, and so a dog can only hope to get a good master. But when the cart reaches the pound, the hitherto silent mongrel demonstrates his contempt for the poodle's philosophy of passive resignation by escaping over the fence, though not without leaving some of his flesh on the nails behind him. We should not exaggerate the revolutionary significance of the tale, as some Soviet critics are inclined to do,[10] but the sense of the allegory is clear: it lies in man's own power to achieve and preserve happiness. The highly individual nature of the mongrel's revolt detracts from any collective revolutionary message the tale may be thought to convey.

Kuprin later became dissatisfied with many of his *Miniatures,* commenting that they contained "a lot of ballast."[11] In 1905 he described them as his "first childish steps along the road of literature," adding that he should hardly be judged by them.[12] Nevertheless, like his *Kiev Types,* the *Miniatures* were all part of his Kiev experience, and marked a further stage in his maturing as a writer.

III *Industrial Sketches*

In the spring and summer of 1896, as a correspondent for the
Kiev papers, Kuprin visited the steel works and coal mines of the
Donbass region north of Rostov-on-Don, now Donetsk Province.
His visit gave rise to four industrial sketches, two published in 1896
— "Rel'soprokatnyi zavod" ("The Rail-Rolling Mill") and
"Yuzovskii zavod" ("The Yuzovsky Works") — and two in 1899,
"V glavnoi shakhte" ("In the Main Shaft") and "V ogne" ("In
the Fire"). He wished to acquaint readers with the processes of
heavy industry and the area in South Russia where it was concentrated, believing most people ignorant of such things. "One must
do justice to us Russians," he wrote, "we know very little of the
interesting places in our native land."[13]

"The Rail-Rolling Mill" reflects his visit to the rail works in
Druzhkovka, north of Donetsk. His technique here is common to
all his industrial sketches: a gradual transition from the general
appearance of the industrial site to the details of its operation.
Beginning with a panoramic view of the works from a distance, a
steam-shrouded vista dominated by tall chimneys belching black
smoke, he takes us nearer, into the smell of coke and the cacophony
of clanking chains, whistling engines, and pounding steam ham-
mers. Then we are led step by step through the rail-making process
in a documentary description that makes almost no mention of the
workers involved. Kuprin's repeated likening of the works and its
machinery to animate creatures points the way to *Moloch*.

Written in the autumn of 1896, "The Yuzovsky Works" is more
ambitious than its predecessor. It describes a visit made by the
author and a companion to a giant steel works and the coal mine
associated with it. Here, in addition to the sounding board of his
companion, Kuprin as narrator uses the device of a loquacious fellow traveler to provide a wealth of information about the works
before the visitors actually reach it. From the traveler we learn the
important facts: the works cover some forty-three thousand acres
and employ about twenty thousand men; the twelve hour working
shifts run from six to six, day and night, all week; the men earn
from sixty kopecks to two roubles a day, and the monthly wage bill
is three hundred thousand roubles. After providing such information and giving a brief account of the development of Yuzovka it-

self, the fellow traveler obligingly alights from the carriage and departs.

A hint of Yuzovka's size is given in the first paragraph, when the travelers see its flickering glow in the night sky twenty versts away. As they draw near, the sight is staggering, "so extraordinary, so immense, so fantastic a panorama that we cried out involuntarily with amazement" (II, 9). The picture is one of incredible confusion and ceaseless activity: mounds of red-hot limestone, dense white and yellow smoke, jets of burning gas, blazing electric lights, clangorous machinery, and huge blast furnaces rearing into the sky "like the turrets of a legendary castle." The murky darkness makes the spectacle appear more awesome still: "It seemed as if a gigantic, apocalyptic wild beast were growling there in the darkness of night, shaking its steel limbs and belching fire" (II, 10).

The narrator visits all sections of the works, describing every stage of production and explaining technical terms either in the text or in footnotes. Their mouths full of sulphurous smoke, their feet burning from the heat of the floor, the visitors comprehend the physical torment of work in such a place. "And we marveled," Kuprin adds, "at the endurance of the men who went on calmly working with their faces almost touching the burning hot metal" (II, 17).

Upon visiting the coal face they find that the miners must work under even worse conditions. Stripped to the waist, crouching in the narrow gallery, they hack coal for twelve hours for a pittance. After only half an hour in the damp darkness of the pit, the visitors are desperate to see the sunlight again. The horrors of the mine, Kuprin infers, would serve as a salutary lesson for all human beings morbidly preoccupied with themselves: "I advise doctors to send absolutely all hypochondriacs, melancholics, neurasthenics, and sick children of the nineteenth century down into the deep mines for half an hour. When they come up, these poor wretches will certainly rejoice at a little piece of green grass lit up by the sun" (II, 22-23).

The later sketches "In the Main Shaft" and "In the Fire," written for the papers *Kiev Word* and *Donskaia rech' (Don Speech)* in 1899, are reworked versions of the two earlier pieces (largely the second of them) with additions from Kuprin's notebooks of 1896. The earlier sketches had pointed to the exploitation of Russian resources by foreign capital and to the presence of Belgians, French, and English in important positions in the Donbass. Linked with this was the neglect of indigenous technical skill by administrators unable to recognize talent. In the later sketches, published three years after *Moloch,* such motifs are developed, and elements of grotesque caricature are employed in the portrayal of foreign engineers. More emphasis is laid too on the exploitation of labor and the appalling conditions in the mines. But, like the first two, these later sketches are still documentary studies of foundry and mine, and Kuprin does not mention active protest by workers, as he does in *Moloch.* Only "In the Fire" contains a hint of unrest in its reference to the use of Circassians as guards because of their reputation for loyalty.

Though very different in emphasis from his sketches of Kiev people, Kuprin's Donbass pieces are not dry industrial guides to steel mills and mines. Like *Kiev Types,* they bear the imprint of the author's personality. Though sometimes involved, his technical descriptions are not tedious because they are so vivid, and Kuprin is careful to vary his pace and tone by easy dialogue, remarks to the reader, and occasional humorous asides. While his visit to the rail mill provokes the thought that, if they have not seen a furnace, the lady pilgrims of Kiev must have a feeble notion of hell, his experiences at Yuzovka lead him to warn the reader amusingly about erratic train services in the area.

All his sketches, whether of city people or industrial plants, reveal Kuprin's burning curiosity about life around him. At the same time, many of them show concern for the plight of the poor or exploited in a hierarchical society, a fact that gives the lie to the opinion, current early in his career, that he was indifferent to social issues. That concern emerged in more elaborate form in *Moloch,* which exposes the injustice inherent in a society where the rouble is king.

IV   Moloch

Written during the summer and autumn of 1896, *Moloch* appeared in the December issue of *Russian Wealth* for that year. Subtitled a *povest',* like "In the Dark," and comparable in length with that work, its structure and cast of characters are more involved and its preoccupations very different. The tale tells of its hero's disquiet at his work for a capitalist industrial enterprise that exploits its employees. After losing the woman he loves to the amoral millionaire who owns that enterprise, the hero suffers a nervous breakdown and is left a broken man.

Thematically *Moloch* belongs firmly in the 1890s, and reflects many of the social and economic issues of that decade. The second half of the 1800s saw the rapid development of Russian capitalism, with its concomitant industrial expansion. As her rail network was enlarged and her textile, metallurgical, and mining industries expanded, Russia's output rose steadily. The All-Russian Industrial Exhibition of 1896 in Nizhny Novgorod, to which Kuprin refers in "The Yuzovsky Works," was designed to demonstrate the impressive achievements of Russian industry.

But with the industrial boom came growing unrest among the new working class, its ranks swelled by poor peasants driven off the land by such agrarian crises as the famine of 1891–1892. The mid-1890s saw the first serious disturbances by industrial workers, while the summer of 1896 witnessed a strike by thirty thousand Petersburg textile operatives. The Donbass had its troubles too, not long before Kuprin visited the area. While 1887 saw a strike by steelworkers in Yuzovka (now Donetsk), August 1892 brought a strike by miners in the region's coalfields. Though not described in Kuprin's industrial sketches, such disturbances are reflected in the workers' revolt at the end of *Moloch*.

Moloch deals with the damaging aspects of Russian capitalism as seen by a sensitive individual caught in the industrial maelstrom of the late 1800s. At the same time it raises other topical issues, such as the social effects of technological progress, the underprivileged position of the working class, the relations between bourgeoisie and intelligentsia, and the latter's role in shaping social change. Through the experience of his hero as a reluctant servant of capitalism in the Donbass, Kuprin points to the social injustice and economic tyranny endemic to newly industrialized Russia.

Though his tale offered rich possibilities for social comment, Kuprin chose instead to focus on the feelings of an individual locked in a personal struggle with an industrial Leviathan that he sees as destructive of human life. It is on the contrast between these forces, one pitifully weak in its isolation, the other boundlessly strong in its power, that the dramatic effect of *Moloch* relies.

Its hero, Andrey Ilich Bobrov, is to some extent an autobiographical character. A progressive *intelligent* of the 1890s, he is shackled by the introspection that occasionally beset Kuprin himself. Though honorable and socially aware, he suffers from the morbid self-scrutiny of Alarin ("In the Dark") and the crippling incapacity for decisive action of Kozlovsky ("The Enquiry"). His

sensitive nature makes him acutely aware of the evils of industrialism, and he can no longer condone a system of which he, as an
engineer, is part. Yet his lack of will renders him incapable of fighting those evils with anything but outbursts of noble indignation.
Though he sympathizes with his fellow men, he is no more than a
"reservoir of social suffering"[14] temperamentally incapable of irri-
gating the parched fields of protest with active help. A late nineteenth century type trapped hopelessly between the hammer of his
convictions and the anvil of his weakness of will, Bobrov traces his
literary ancestry to the pages of Chekhov, whose characters often
find contact with reality too painful an experience to bear.

Kuprin devotes considerable space to portraying his hero's states
of mind, a concern underlined, as the Soviet scholar Pavel Berkov
shows, by his frequent use of the verb "to feel" (*chuvstvovat'*) and
verbs akin to it.[15] Subject to insomnia and nervous exhaustion,
Bobrov is prone to depression, while his "gentle, almost feminine
nature" suffers cruelly from the buffeting of everyday life. He is so
acutely sensitive that he likens himself to "a man who has been
skinned alive." Kuprin's description of his face emphasizes his
gentleness and innate goodness, but also reveals his intense
thoughtfulness and nervous instability: "His large, white, beautiful
forehead ... attracted one's attention most of all. His dilated
pupils ... were so large that his eyes seemed black, not grey. His
thick, uneven eyebrows met at the bridge of his nose, lending his
eyes a severe, intent, seemingly ascetic expression. [His] lips were
nervous and thin ... the right corner of his mouth was a little
higher than the left; his moustache and beard were small, sparse,
whitish, and quite boyish.... When Bobrov laughed, his eyes
became gentle and gay and his whole face became attractive"
(11, 72).

Details of his biography, provided only in the first (journal) version of *Moloch,* helped explain Bobrov's instability. He was
brought up with abundant tenderness by his mother, who later
became deranged and fell victim to religious mania. Kuprin deleted
this section, with its clear hint of predisposition to psychological
disorder, so that Bobrov's neurasthenia should appear purely the
result of his traumatic involvement with industrialism. The preoccupation with abnormal states of mind that Kuprin had shown in
his earliest works had revealed itself once more, as he himself was
quick to see. In a letter to Mikhailovsky he wrote: "I've still not
managed to avoid morbid psychology. Perhaps this unhappy genre
is inseparable from me?"[16]

Bobrov's personality is sketched in Chapter I, but not until the industrialist Kvashnin arrives at Ivankovo in Chapter VI and touches off the plot does the story acquire dramatic force. The first five chapters paint the industrial backcloth of the work, present its secondary characters, and heighten the atmosphere of expectation before Kvashnin appears. Much of Chapter I is devoted to a panoramic view of the works as Bobrov walks toward them, a picture to be complemented in Chapter V by the description of the site from a distance (drawn from "The Yuzovsky Works"), and in Chapter VII by the detailed account of production processes. Sprawling over fifty square versts, the plant is a city of buildings, furnaces, and railways, ringing with a chaos of sound and draped with a pall of white lime dust. But what distinguishes this vista from those already seen in Kuprin's industrial sketches is the detailed attention he gives to the myriad workers Bobrov sees on the site: "Human toil seethed here like a huge, complex, precise machine. Thousands of men — engineers, bricklayers, mechanics, carpenters, metal workers, excavators, joiners, and blacksmiths — had gathered . . . to give up . . . their strength, health, mind, and energy so industrial progress could take one step forward" (II, 74). As he walks through the rail-rolling shop, Bobrov notices the workers' "pale faces dirty with coal and parched by fire," and feels part of their physical suffering. "Then," Kuprin adds, "he felt ashamed of his well-cared for appearance, his fine linen and his salary of three thousand a year . . ."

Chapters II and III show some of Bobrov's colleagues, people of his own class who willingly serve the industrial colossus for gain. In brief strokes through his conversation with Bobrov, Kuprin depicts the loathsome careerist Svezhevsky. With his ingratiating stoop, his insinuating gossip, and his obsequious language full of cloying diminutives, Svezhevsky is a latter-day Uriah Heep, constantly giggling and rubbing his damp, cold hands. He it is who first mentions Kvashnin. In servile adulation, he tells Bobrov of the great man's power and influence, giving us a glimpse of Kvashnin before he arrives and arousing Bobrov's antipathy for this repugnant demigod, who receives two hundred thousand roubles for attending seven meetings a year.

Next we encounter Zinenko, in charge of stores at the works. For all his easy geniality, this pushing character fawns on his superiors, gossips about his colleagues, and tyrannizes his subordinates. Of his five daughters, only Nina is beautiful, a curious fact that,

Kuprin hints darkly, only Mme Zinenko could explain. With her aristocratic hands and fluffy hair, Nina is the hope of her philistine family, who think only of money. Believing himself in love with her, Bobrov cannot see through her beguiling charm to her spiritually atrophied soul. Though attracted to her physically, he cannot bring himself to propose because he is growing increasingly aware of the differences in attitude between them. His disquiet is intensified by the contrast between the longing he feels when he is away from her and the frustration she and her family arouse in him when he is among them. His feelings for Nina reach a crisis at the end of Chapter IV. Repelled by her rapture at the mention of Kvashnin's wealth, he angrily takes his leave, convinced that in a world where all serve Mammon even Nina has her price.

Apart from Bobrov, the only character sympathetically portrayed in these early chapters is the Jewish doctor Goldberg, the works physician and the hero's only close friend. More of a silhouette than a flesh and blood creation, he is a sounding board for Bobrov's views.[17] Though close to Bobrov in his humane attitudes, Goldberg is less pessimistic. In Chapter V, through these two men, Kuprin offers opposite responses to the topical issue of technological progress. Convinced of the harmfulness of his work, Bobrov attacks scientific progress, whereas Goldberg believes that on balance it is both desirable and beneficial.

In publicistic tones hitherto uncharacteristic of Kuprin, Bobrov calculates the cost of such progress in human lives — the most telling part of his argument. It is generally agreed, he says, that work in the mines and steel industry shortens a man's life by approximately a quarter. This means the worker gives his employer three months of his life a year, a week a month, or six hours a day. The thirty thousand men at this plant alone, he goes on, give one hundred and eighty thousand hours of their lives every twenty-four hours, a figure roughly equivalent to twenty years every twenty-four hours. In view of the fact that few workers live beyond forty, Bobrov concludes, the industrial giant consumes a whole man every two days. Horrified by his own figures, he sees an analogy between voracious industry and the dread gods of biblical times who devoured human beings offered in sacrifice. The frenzied industrial expansion of Russia has resurrected Moloch, the brazen god of the Ammonites for whom children were made "to pass through the fire" in ritual sacrifice (2 Kings 23:10). Flinging open the window to view the awesome spectacle of the works ablaze in the night,

Bobrov cries: "Here he is — Moloch, who demands warm human blood! Remember how they cast women, children and slaves into his fiery belly when the god demanded food!... Bring him your sacrifice and worship him, you benefactors of the human race..."[18] This is the cost of progress as Bobrov sees it, the ceaseless sacrifice of lives to the insatiable idol of capitalism, who corrupts or destroys all who serve him.

The arrival of Kvashnin in Chapter VI acts as a catalyst on the various characters, making them openly adopt the attitudes already suggested in them by Kuprin. While Kvashnin's presence reveals his minions in all their sycophancy, his person becomes for Bobrov the very embodiment of industrial amorality. If Bobrov is revealed from within, his antipode Kvashnin is shown only from without, a loathsome but flat representation of capitalist excess. Gluttonous, debauched, monstrously fat, he will pay any price to satisfy his merest whim. His insatiable appetites and his limitless power over all who serve him make him in Bobrov's eyes the incarnation of ruthless greed — Moloch himself. But the identification of the two is not immediate, and Kuprin uses the process whereby Bobrov gradually arrives at it to convey his increasingly tortured state of mind. We first see Kvashnin in his railway carriage as it pulls into Ivankovo station. A grotesque, eyeless monster, he sits "with his colossal legs apart and his belly bulging out." Beneath his round hat "gleamed his fiery hair," while his "clean-shaven face with its flabby cheeks and triple chin ... looked sleepy and displeased" (II, 103). As he lowers his vast bulk onto the platform, he looks to Bobrov like "a coarsely made Japanese idol" (II, 104). The idea of Kvashnin as a god who demands human sacrifice is reinforced in Chapter IX, where the weeping wives of workers hold out their infants to him in supplication. But not until the end, in Chapter XI, is the identification of Kvashnin and Moloch complete. Here Kvashnin becomes both the personification and (through his biblical likeness) the dehumanized symbol of capitalism itself. When, during the picnic, news arrives of a revolt by workers at the factory, the guests panic. As Kvashnin's troika, illumined by its flickering lantern, whirls away into the darkness, it seems to Bobrov that it is not Kvashnin driving by, but "some blood-stained, ugly, terrible deity like those idols of eastern cults under whose chariots fanatics ... hurl themselves during religious processions" (II, 137).

At the elaborate picnic for his Ivankovo colleagues, Kvashnin is exposed as the proud ideologist of capitalist progress and the unashamed manipulator of human lives. Addressing the guests, he praises those, like himself, who engineer the industrial development of Russia and the world: "Hold our banner high. Don't forget we are the salt of the earth, that the future belongs to us.... Have we not enmeshed the globe with a network of railways? Do we not open wide the bowels of the earth and transform her treasures into guns, bridges, locomotives, rails and colossal machines? Do we not, by the strength of our genius, bring movement to thousands of millions of capital?" (II, 134). Shortly afterward, Kvashnin announces the marriage of Nina and Svezhevsky, an arrangement that enables him to have Nina as his mistress under a cloak of respectability. Like all the rest, Nina has been suborned by the rouble.

Bobrov's fundamental weakness of will emerges with painful clarity in the closing chapter, during the verbal struggle between himself and his "double." The hitherto latent split in his personality now manifests itself as the result of the crisis within him. His emotions are a conflicting mixture: jealousy at losing the girl he loves, anger at what Kvashnin has done to get her, disgust at her readiness to become Kvashnin's mistress for gain, and despair at the loneliness he anticipates. Two different voices now speak in him. While his own voice demands decisive action against Kvashnin, the voice of "the other" jeeringly resists it. As Bobrov wanders alone through the works at dawn, the two voices vie for supremacy. When his own voice suggests suicide as a way of escape from his torment, "...the other, *the stranger,* retorted...: "No, you won't kill yourself.... You're too faint-hearted to do it...."

"What am I to do then?" whispered Andrey Ilich....

"If you hate Kvashnin so much, then go and kill him."

"I will kill him!" cried Bobrov, stopping and raising his fists in fury....

But the *other* remarked with venomous mockery: "But you won't kill him.... You haven't the determination or the strength to do it...." " (II, 142).

Bobrov's own voice prevails temporarily, and feeling the need for decisive action, he decides to blow up the factory boilers by stoking them over the limit. But as the boiler pressure rises dangerously, he is exhausted by the unaccustomed work of shoveling coal, and his burst of feverish energy subsides. Now his *other* inner voice speaks mockingly for the last time, and finally triumphs: " "Well, go on then, you've only got to make one more movement! But you won't ... and tomorrow you won't even dare admit you wanted to blow up the boilers last night" " (II, 143). Like Kozlovsky's outburst at the end of "The Enquiry," Bobrov's frenzy ends in emotional prostration. In the closing lines of the tale, he begs Goldberg for the morphia that will enable him to escape himself.

For all that *Moloch* deals with the damaging effects of industrial progress, Kuprin devotes very little space to the factory's workers. Though their plight is revealed convincingly enough in statistical terms during the argument between Goldberg and Bobrov, nowhere in the work are they more than a faceless mass drifting uncertainly on the periphery of the action. In the rare instances when they are shown in any detail, it is in crowd scenes witnessed through the hero's eyes. While there are hints of the workers' strength and skill, these qualities are not developed; instead, their dominant characteristics are submissiveness and resignation. Nowhere is this more obvious than during the service of dedication for the new blast furnace, attended by three thousand workers. Dividing the crowd up with his eye into its different *groups* of workmen (masons, casters, smiths and laborers), Bobrov perceives "something elemental and mighty, and at the same time touching and childlike" in the praying of this "vast grey mass." "And in whom," he reflects, "if not in Our Lady alone are these big children with their steadfast, simple hearts to trust, these meek warriors who every day leave their dank, chill mud huts for their customary feat of endurance and courage?" (II, 107).

But the workers' revolt in the finale shows that, contrary to Bobrov's belief, their endurance has its limits. Though for the moment disorganized and uncontrolled, they are an immense force that one day will smash the tyranny of Moloch-Kvashnin forever. Though it subsides as rapidly as it flares up, the revolt is the first sign of the terrible nemesis to come.

It is interesting that the manuscript of *Moloch* submitted to *Russian Wealth* contained more explicit description of the revolt than the final version. But at Mikhailovsky's request reference to the revolt was toned down, a measure dictated perhaps by his fear of censorship or his dislike, as a Neo-Populist, of the idea of a violent workers' uprising. Whatever the reasons for them, Mikhailovsky's changes weakened the denouement of *Moloch* severely. Relegated to the background again, the workers become the faceless mass they were earlier in the tale, a dimly threatening bulk stalking the fringes of the plot. Without leaders or individualized participants, their revolt is reduced to nothing more than an atmosphere of vague tension pervading the closing pages. As Kuprin wrote to Mikhailovsky upon altering his manuscript: "About the revolt — not a word. One will only be able to feel it."[19]

The defects of *Moloch* are several. The melodrama of works like "In the Dark" emerges again, especially in the Bobrov-Nina-Kvashnin triangle, which bears some resemblance to the earlier Alarin-Zinaida-Kashperov pattern. Two sections of *Moloch* are unashamedly sensational: the fevered verbal exchanges between Bobrov and Mme Zinenko at the picnic, and the arrival of the hero, blood-stained and tattered, at the hospital to beg Goldberg for morphia. While the identification of Kvashnin with Moloch is a powerful unifying device lending splendid impetus to the plot, Kuprin's use of grotesque hyperbole in the portrayal of Kvashnin verges on caricature. As if aware of this, he carefully stresses Kvashnin's grace and agility as he dances with Nina at the picnic, a glimpse of a hitherto unsuspected facet that lightens the otherwise unrelieved portrayal of him as a gargantuan monster. A similar effect is achieved in the scene where Kvashnin pacifies the workers' womenfolk clamoring around him, a scene Berkov describes as "tragi-comic."[20] Of the handful of individualized characters in the work, two in particular suffer from underdevelopment — the cardboardlike Goldberg and the episodic Belgian engineer Andrea. Well-educated and highly intelligent, the latter is a promising figure intriguingly introduced but then left in limbo. Skeptical and disillusioned, this outwardly imperturbable man hides his despair at the fruitlessness of his existence under a mask of sarcastic cynicism. Finding solace in drink as the hero does in morphia, Andrea is just as much a victim of Moloch as Bobrov. Perhaps the major deficiency of the tale, however, is its lack of consistent pace and polish. An excess of technical detail in the sketch-like sections (especially in Chapter VII) retards the narrative and diverts attention from the work's primary concern. Probably because of the damage Mikhailovsky did to the initial text, the conclusion lacks power. In his attempt to convey the rapid sequence of events after the revolt is announced, Kuprin creates an impressionistic series of swiftly flitting scenes that culminate in an unsatisfying and hurried ending.

Kuprin was not the first writer of his time to take up the theme of capitalist progress. While authors before him — Ivan Goncharov, for example — had praised the drive and resourcefulness of the rising capitalist class, others — Nikolay Nekrasov, Mikhail Saltykov-

Shchedrin, Alexey Pisemsky — had shown capitalism as a destructive social force, and depicted the moral disintegration of people attacked by the bacillus of money. Nor was Kuprin the first to depict capitalism as a voracious idol devouring human lives, though perhaps only Zola had equaled the horrendous image-symbol of Moloch. Only two years after Kuprin, Chekhov would use a similar parallel, when in his tale "A Case History" (1898) he described capitalist industry as "that monster with the blood-red eyes, that devil who ruled everyone — bosses and workers alike — deceiving one and all."[21]

Moloch's originality lies in the clarity with which its central image reveals the price of industrial progress. The argument between Goldberg and Bobrov that gives rise to that image is pivotal to the work, and examines problems that concerned Kuprin himself. While it is hard to see how Kuprin could agree altogether with his hero's rejection of technological progress, Bobrov's view would seem to be one the author broadly shares. As the denouement shows, Kuprin appears at this stage to condone the use of force by workers to resist exploitation, a point stressed by Soviet critics. The value he set at the time on positive opposition to oppression is underlined by the mongrel's philosophy of active resistance in "Dogs' Happiness," published in September 1896, when *Moloch* was nearing completion.

Nevertheless, the prime aim of *Moloch* is not to advocate revolutionary industrial agitation of the kind shown later in Gorky's novel *The Mother* (1907). Concerned primarily with the feelings vis-à-vis capitalist industry of an intellectual who takes no active steps to improve the workers' lot, *Moloch* is, as Berkov neatly puts it, a "socio-psychological" rather than a "socio-political" work.[22] Since some Soviet critics tend to exaggerate the revolutionary tendency of *Moloch,* it is instructive to note that in no work after it did Kuprin ever portray the industrial working class in any detail. Indeed, only two later works are at all reminiscent of *Moloch* in theme or situation. The tale "Putanitsa" ("A Muddle," 1897) has in its hero, Pchelovodov, a figure akin to Bobrov. Once a technician at a foundry, he is committed to an asylum by the machinations of his employer after arguing with him over fines imposed on workers. Situationally closer to *Moloch* is the story "V nedrakh zemli" ("In the Bowels of the Earth," 1899), which describes the appalling conditions in the mines and the heroism of its boy hero in saving a fellow miner's life. But neither work displays the degree of social commitment evident in *Moloch,* and in both Kuprin is more interested in the behavior of his hero than in the social problems of an industrial society. On this basis one is tempted to conclude that his concern for the industrial worker in *Moloch* was little more than a passing phase.

V The Polesye Cycle

The later 1890s saw Kuprin engaged in many of the temporary occupations that make his biography so fascinating The year 1897 took him first to Volhynia Province in the northwest Ukraine, where he worked as an estate manager, and then to the Polesye area in southern Belorussia, where he helped to grow *makhorka,* an inferior tobacco.[23] The winter of 1897–1898 took him to Ryazan Province, where he hunted and worked on the tale *Olesya.* By 1898 he was in Odessa again, while 1899 and 1900 took him through southern Russia — Rostov, Novocherkassk, Taganrog, Tsaritsyn, and Novorossiisk. Throughout these years he continued to contribute tales and sketches to papers in Kiev and elsewhere.

Unlike his months in the Donbass, the rich experience of these years was reflected time and again in his writing. As an antidote to the poison of industrial civilization that he had found so repugnant in *Moloch,* the timeless Russian countryside imprinted itself on his memory and remained a wellspring of inspiration for the rest of his life. In the 1920s he wrote that his months in the forests of Polesye and Ryazan had been the most beneficial of his life: "There I absorbed my most vigorous, noble, extensive, and fruitful impressions. And ... I came to know the Russian language and landscape."[24]

His impressions of his stay in Polesye are the basis of his unfinished "Polesye cycle," published between 1898 and 1901. Consisting of three tales — "Lesnaia glush'" ("The Backwoods"), *Olesya,* and "Oboroten'" ("The Werewolf") — the cycle is linked thematically with the later forest sketch "Na glukharei" ("Hunting Wood Grouse," 1899) and the story "Boloto" ("The Swamp," 1902). Published in *Russian Wealth* in September 1898, "The Backwoods" was intended as the first work in the cycle, to be followed by *Olesya.* But neither *Olesya* nor "The Werewolf" was accepted by the journal, and Kuprin was obliged to place them elsewhere. While the first was serialized in *The Kievan* in 1898, the second was published in *Odesskie Novosti (Odessa News)* in 1901, a delay that may explain why the cycle was then left incomplete. The Polesye tales depend on the contrast between town and country. The hypocrisy and corruption of the urban environment stand out in ugly relief against the natural beauty of the countryside and the spiritual purity of its people. Intended as the opening tale of the cycle, "The Backwoods" is a sketchlike ethnographical piece designed to depict the human beings who inhabit this pristine environment. In its distanced, rather documentary revelation of peasant types, it recalls Turgenev's *Sketches from a Hunter's Album* of half a century before. The physical and temperamental contrast drawn here between the characters of Kirila and Talimon echoes that between Khor and Kalinych in Turgenev's first sketch. Kirila, the efficient but obsequious village police assistant, is a luckless hunter portrayed with undisguised irony. Talimon, on the other hand, enjoys the author's full sympathy. Though lazy and disorganized, this shy man is an excellent shot and thoroughly at home in the forest, where he has spent most of his life. Kuprin extends the contrast even to his characters' dogs: whereas Kirila's hound is noisy, impulsive, and ingratiating, Talimon's is silent, cautious, and indifferent to all gestures of affection.

The ending of the tale brings an abrupt change of mood. After an evocative scene of grouse hunting in the stillness of early dawn, news comes that the peasant Alexander has killed his unfaithful wife with an axe. While this occurrence confirms the narrator and his friends in their belief that the town where the woman became debauched is a place of corruption, it also shows that not even the primordial vastnesses of rural Russia are free from violence. Nor are their inhabitants always models of spiritual purity. Seeing the noisy villagers gathered round the murderer, the narrator walks quickly by, "away from this hateful crowd that always flocks with such loathsome eagerness to blood, filth, and carrion" (II, 310).

Folk tales and legends are as much a part of life in Polesye as the all-encompassing forest. Some of them are so fantastic that they seem to spring, not from the superstitious folk of this remote region, but from the age-old forest itself. It is Talimon, the agile spirit of the woods with his black eyes and black beard, who tells the author the story of the buzzard condemned by God to drink only raindrops from leaves, and of the young Cossack, Opanas, destroyed by the greed of a cruel miller's daughter. The much shorter "Werewolf," subtitled "A Polesye Legend," tells of young Stetsko, who returns from war transformed into a werewolf who leads his pack against travelers in the forest at night. In an effort to convey the original flavor of the legends as he heard them, Kuprin carefully preserves the local speech peculiarities of his characters. Linguistically, "The Backwoods" is the richest tale of the cycle; when it first appeared, Kuprin supplied translations for local words in footnotes.[25] Yet despite Kuprin's restraint, Talimon's speech — a colorful blend of Russian, Belorussian, and Ukrainian — becomes tiresome in places.

Olesya is the most charming of Kuprin's rural tales. Though meant at first to be only part of the Polesye cycle, this poetic story of the love between an urban intellectual and a beautiful country girl expanded into a full novelette of a significance far surpassing that of the other regional tales. It is also autobiographical: "All this happened to me,"[26] Kuprin wrote mysteriously toward the end of his life. The story was always one of his favorites. Referring once to both *Olesya* and his later work "The River of Life," he said: "Here there is life, freshness ... more of my soul ... than in my other tales."[27]

The first (newspaper) version of the work, subtitled "From Memories of Volhynia," appeared with an introduction claiming that the story was told by the now elderly Ivan Timofeevich Poroshin, as he recalled his youthful love for the "real Polesye sorceress" Olesya many years ago. Kuprin removed the introduction in later versions, and so heightened the dramatic impact of his tale by increasing its immediacy and preventing the reader from learning the outcome in advance.

Olesya's introductory chapter reveals little about the people and customs of Polesye. Instead, Kuprin contents himself with a humorous account of the narrator's futile attempts to doctor the peasants and of the disastrous writing lessons he gives to Yarmola, his servant and hunting companion. In the second chapter, the conversation between Yarmola and the narrator turns to witches and witchcraft. Relying on the information provided by its predecessor, "The Backwoods," *Olesya* assumes the reader is familiar with Polesye and its people, and thus focuses on the relationship between hero and heroine.

The narrator, Ivan Timofeevich, is a shadowy but attractive figure whose ready irony at his own expense endears him to us. Instead of restorative peace, Polesye brings him only intolerable boredom, from which the prospect of meeting a real witch offers a welcome diversion. Akin to Kozlovsky and Bobrov before him,

Timofeevich is a noble-hearted but weak-willed urban animal whose hesitant nature contrasts sharply with the bold decisiveness of Olesya's rural temperament. His relations with Olesya teach both him and us more about him. With the uncanny accuracy of the fortuneteller she is, Olesya characterizes him neatly: "...though you're a good man, you're weak ... not a man of your word" (II, 332). And indeed, irresolution remains the dominant trait of his character. Vacillating between his desire to marry Olesya and his feeling that their relationship must end, by default he leaves the decision to her. She takes it, and leaves forever.

If Kuprin describes Timofeevich in some detail in his first few pages, he surrounds Olesya with an aura of fascinating mystery. All we learn before we meet her in Chapter III is that she came as a child from the north with her grandmother, old Manuilikha, later driven from the village as a witch. Brought up in the remote forests, she is untouched by civilization. While Manuilikha is almost a Baba Yaga figure — the traditional witch of Russian fairy tales — Olesya is an idealized, romantic creation, the archetypal daughter of nature, as beautiful and free as the virgin forests to which she belongs. Exquisitely charming in love, she becomes proudly resolute at moments of crisis, exhibiting a native wisdom that dismays the flabby Timofeevich. Designed to suggest her soul rather than reveal her outward form, Olesya's appearance is only lightly sketched, sufficiently detailed for us to picture her yet insubstantial enough for us to form our own subjective image of her. The beauty of her face, Kuprin writes, lay "in those big, dark, shining eyes to which the slender eyebrows lent an elusive hint of slyness, imperiousness, and naiveté, ... and in the willful curve of her lips, of which the lower one ... pushed forward with a determined, obstinate look" (II, 325). Delightfully attractive as she is, Olesya is a mysterious creature acutely sensitive to the ever-changing moods of the forest around her. Her oneness with the wild beauty of nature lends her supernatural powers that Timofeevich finds disturbing and sinister. In thrall to the dark forces deep in her soul, possessed of "that instinctive, obscure, strange knowledge mingled with wild superstition and passed down from generation to generation like the closest secret" (II, 343), she possesses the gifts of prophecy and hypnosis, and can unerringly foretell death. All this she combines with an engagingly practical common sense that makes her reject without hesitation Timofeevich's talk of marriage: "Well what sort of wife would I be to you? ... I can't even read and I don't know

how to behave.... You'd have nothing but boundless shame
because of me..." (II, 363).
    Nature is at the center of *Olesya* just as it is the lifeblood of the
heroine herself. A living part of this world where she knows only
the stillness of forest, marsh and immense, embracing sky, she is
inconceivable anywhere else. In his heart of hearts Timofeevich
knows this too. When he imagines her as his wife, he recognizes the
absurdity of Olesya in a fashionable dress talking to the wives of his
colleagues in an urban drawing room, torn forever from "this
ancient forest full of mysterious powers and legends" (II, 361).
Summoning up her image, he sees his beloved as an integral part of
the natural kingdom in which she has her being, "her young body
grown as shapely and strong as young fir trees in the freedom of the
old pine forest" (II, 329). But never is nature a mere static backcloth in *Olesya,* an inert prop to the story's action. Instead, it is an
independent actor in the drama played out by hero and heroine, a
force that, as the early Soviet critic Vorovsky puts it, "lives its own
life and pays no need to man."[28] Polesye's quietly insistent beauty
is the inspiration for the love of hero and heroine, and it is with
nature's festive though silent approval that they declare that love:
"And all that night merged into some magic, enchanting fairytale.
The moon rose and with its radiance illumined the forest with fantastic, mysterious light of many hues, casting amidst the darkness
uneven, pale bluish patches on the gnarled tree trunks, the curved
branches, and the moss soft as a plush carpet. The slender trunks of
birches showed up white and distinct, while on their sparse foliage
were flung translucent, silver cloaks of gauze. Here and there the
light did not penetrate at all beneath the dense canopy of pine
branches. Complete, impenetrable darkness was there, and only in
its very center did a ray of light, slipping in from who knows where,
suddenly brightly illumine a long row of trees and fling onto the
ground a straight, narrow path so bright, elegant, and charming
that it looked like an avenue decorated by elves for a ceremonial
procession by Oberon and Titania. And embracing one another we
walked on without a word amidst this smiling, living legend, over-
whelmed by our happiness and the awesome silence of the forest"
(II, 359).
    The concordance between the moods of man and events in the
natural world lends dramatic force to *Olesya.* Timofeevich's feelings run in close parallel to changes of season throughout the work,
a device that not only enables Kuprin to vary the narrative tension

of his story but also underlines the tragic inevitability of its outcome. The beginning finds Timofeevich lonely and bored amid the lifeless winter landscape of Polesye. Then early spring, with its jubilant birds and abundant water, fills him with premonitions of love. A month in high summer brings his relationship with Olesya to passionate fullness, a month when "like a pagan god or a strong, young animal, he reveled in light, warmth, conscious joie de vivre and calm, healthy, sensual love" (II, 360). But the lowering skies of autumn bring the destructive hailstorm of the closing chapter, a grim presage that his love is doomed.

Despite Kuprin's removal of the introduction from the first version of *Olesya,* we are left in no doubt that the story is a memoir. Several references by Timofeevich to the memories left by his Polesye experience remind us that these are the recollections of an old man looking back with nostalgia to the love of his youth. The episode in which the villagers attempt to tar Olesya makes the point again, and more forcefully. Timofeevich describes it, not through his own eyes (for he was not there), but through those of two episodic characters who witnessed it, a clerk from a nearby estate and a forester's wife, who gives her account two months later. This double distancing device heightens the aura of perspective that surrounds Timofeevich's remembrance of things past. The closing lines of *Olesya* clearly reaffirm its memoir quality. In the forest hut now deserted forever by Manuilikha and Olesya, Timofeevich's eye falls upon a string of cheap red beads hanging at the window — "the only thing I had left as a keepsake of Olesya and her tender, generous love" (II, 381).

Though there is some truth in Chekhov's unflattering view of *Olesya* as mere "naive romanticism,"[29] the story remains one of Kuprin's best. Framed by the quietly evocative beauty of Polesye, his miraculous heroine stands out in brilliant relief against the somber hostility around her. The narrator's memory of her "tender, generous love" became an abiding motif in Kuprin's later work, rising to its crescendo in the gorgeously lyrical *Sulamif (Sulamith,* 1908), then fading softly through the sadly elegiac "Granatovyi braslet" ("The Bracelet of Garnets," 1911) into the poignant resignation of *Koleso vremeni (The Wheel of Time,* 1929).

Moloch and *Olesya* set the seal on Kuprin's reputation, and in late 1901 he joined the *Journal for All* in Petersburg. Like his resignation from the army, the move to Petersburg was a climacteric in his career. His years as a journalist had brought him vast experience

of permanent value for his work. Now those years were over, and
armed with what they had taught him, Kuprin joined the literary
circles of the capital.

CHAPTER 3

Petersburg

I Literary Acquaintances

THE first years of the new century were the most important of
Kuprin's career. No longer cut off from literary colleagues, he
found himself in the center of Russian cultural life, rubbing shoulders with foremost writers of the day. The early 1900s saw the
formation of several friendships important for his literary development. Brief though it was, one of the most vital was that with
Chekhov. Between 1901 and Chekhov's death in 1904, the two men
met several times and corresponded regularly.[1] Kuprin sought
Chekhov's advice on his work and discussed social and political
matters with him. These years also saw the beginning of Kuprin's
friendship with Ivan Bunin, which would last almost forty years,
continuing while both were in emigration.[2] Also important was his
intimate friendship with the scholar and critic F. D. Batyushkov of
God's World. For several years after 1905, Kuprin would visit his
remote estate of Danilovskoe, near Ustyuzhna in Vologda Province.[3] They wrote to each other frequently, and the one hundred
and fifty surviving letters are only part of their correspondence.[4]
Some credit for Kuprin's success in these years must go to Mirolyubov of the *Journal for All.* Aware that Kuprin was not given to systematic work, he insisted that he give his writing driving purpose-
fulness, a quality readily apparent in Kuprin's tales of the early
1900s. Kuprin later recalled Mirolyubov's guidance with great
gratitude, though he disapproved of his editor's flirtation with the
right wing "Religio-philosophical Society" in Petersberg.[5] In
November of 1902 Kuprin met Gorky for the second time (they had
first met in 1900 in Yalta.) Gorky would exert an incalculable influence on Kuprin's career, and especially on *The Duel.*[6] Later on,

Kuprin openly acknowledged his debt to him: "To Gorky I owe a very great deal. He not only had a sincere and attentive regard for me and my work, but also --- made me think about things I had not thought about before. My contact with him is of enormous significance to me."[7]

In 1901 Kuprin joined the Moscow literary society *Sreda (Wednesday)*, founded in 1899 by the writer Nikolay Teleshov. An extension of a group dating from the mid-1880s, it was composed chiefly of realist writers of the younger generation, among whom were Gorky, Bunin, and Leonid Andreev. In 1903 the *Znanie (Knowledge)* publishing concern founded by Gorky began to publish its collections of tales by contemporary writers. The first comprised works written mainly by members of the *Wednesday* group.

In October of 1902, *Knowledge* offered to publish a collection of Kuprin's tales. Guided by Gorky, Kuprin chose his best works for the book, revising them with scrupulous care and omitting even the sparkling "Allez!" because it seemed out of place. When in February 1903 the collection of eight tales appeared — among them "The Enquiry" and *Moloch* — Kuprin was immensely pleased. To be published by *Knowledge* was high recommendation for any writer. "It's pleasant," he wrote to Chekhov, "to come out into the world under such a flag."[8] Tolstoy praised the collection for its vivid language,[9] and distinguished critics were almost unanimous in their approbation, pointing to Kuprin's closeness in themes and technique to Chekhov and Gorky. Angel Bogdanovich of *God's World* — who in 1897 had written unflatteringly of *Moloch* — now praised Kuprin's compact style and his ability to convey a feeling of effervescent joie de vivre.[10] Gorky himself, writing to Teleshov in March of 1903, about future contributors to *Knowledge,* ranked Kuprin third, after Chekhov and Andreev.[11]

Despite the social and literary success of Kuprin's first years in Petersburg, the period also had its drawbacks. His employment with *God's World* left him little time for his own writing, and when his work did appear in that journal, malicious tongues whispered that he owed his success to his family connections. "Life is hard," he wrote to a friend in Kiev, "scandal, gossip, envy, hatred ... I'm very lonely and sad."[12] A violent disagreement with his colleague Bogdanovich proved the last straw, and in February 1904 Kuprin left the journal altogether.

Because of his editorial work, Kuprin wrote less between 1902 and 1905 than he had in the provinces. But if the quantity of his writing was reduced — some twenty tales in all — its quality was incomparably higher. Gone were the melodramatic elements of his earlier tales, with their penchant for the abnormal. More conscious now of the blatant contrasts prevalent in Russian society, he turned his attention to the plight of the "little man," thus following the best traditions of Russian literature.

II "At the Circus"

Published in *God's World* in January, 1902, "At the Circus" was clear proof of Kuprin's literary maturity. Successful among readers and critics alike, it brought high praise from both Chekhov and Tolstoy. Writing to Olga Knipper soon after its publication, Chekhov described the tale as "a free, ingenuous, talented piece written . . . by . . . an expert."[13] Kuprin never ceased to love the circus all his life. He felt boundless admiration for the skill and daring of performers who daily risk their lives to entertain their audience. At the same time he was attracted by the camaraderie of polyglot circus folk, closely knit by the traditions of their profession and proud of their individual skills, handed down from one generation to the next. While working on the tale, Kuprin commented that, though its plot was simple, it offered him tremendous creative scope: "the circus during rehearsals in the daytime and a performance at night, jargon, customs, the description of a wrestling match, straining muscles and beautiful poses, the excitement of the crowd, and so on."[14]

As Kuprin said, the plot of the work is delightfully simple. The wrestler Arbuzov (based on a performer of that name whom Kuprin had met in Odessa) feels unwell before his final bout with the American Reber, enters the ring against his doctor's advice, loses, and dies immediately afterward of a heart attack. While Kuprin's earlier circus works ("Lolli," "Allez!" and the play *The Clown*) had focused on such sensational incidents as catastrophes and suicides, here Arbuzov's death is conveyed in a calm, matter-of-fact manner. "Everything vanished," Kuprin concludes his tale, "thought, consciousness, pain, and anguish. And it was just as simple and quick as if someone had blown on a candle burning in a dark room and put it out. . . (II, 173).

Arbuzov's physical strength is pivotal to the story, and heightens the tragedy of his premature death. In the opening scene, the circus physician Lukhovitsyn admires Arbuzov's magnificent physique, wondering at the wrestler's "huge, sleek, shining, pale pink body

with ... its muscles jutting out sharply as hard as wood"
(III, 147). The details of Arbuzov's illness which follow were supplied by Chekhov while Kuprin was staying with him in Yalta in the
summer of 1901. The wrestler, Lukhovitsyn explains, is suffering
from hypertrophy of the heart, or *cor bovinum,* a condition afflicting many who engage in very strenuous exertion. Arbuzov's physical magnificence is emphasized not only through the picture of the
hunchbacked doctor prodding him in admiration, but also through
the unattractive circus director, "a small, stout, thin-legged man
with hunched shoulders," whose bulldog face reminds one of Bis-
marck (III, 158).

Arbuzov is the victim of the circus system, which revolves round
money and takes no account of individuals in its service. But, on a
higher level, for circus we may read any rigid system based on
money that ignores the little man. Kuprin's criticism is levelled at
the circus director's ruthless indifference to his artists' needs: since
he knows that cancellation of the bout will reduce his takings, he
refuses to put it off. Forced to perform, the wrestler feels "some
nameless, merciless power" (III, 169) driving him into the ring,
even as he becomes acutely aware of how "absurd, useless, ridiculous, and brutal" his performance will be. Once out before the
audience, he feels hopelessly trapped in the bright circle of light, as
if "someone else's enormous will had brought him here and no
power could make him turn back" (III, 170). He is gripped by the
instinctive horror felt by the ox as it is led into the slaughterhouse.
His sense of inexorable doom is intensified by the word "boomer-
ang" ringing unaccountably again and again in his head and symbolizing the cyclical nature of all men's lives. As his own life comes
full circle, the word echoes once more in his mind before he is swal-
lowed by oblivion.

What gives "At the Circus" such power is the skill with which
Kuprin conveys Arbuzov's feelings as they rise from vague disquiet
in the opening chapter, through feverish sickness in his room, to a
crescendo of impotent horror just before the bout. Conveyed in
taut language that becomes more charged as the tale progresses, his
suffering is set delicately into the more relaxed frame of circus
activity with its varied characters engaged in their rehearsals, such
colorful figures as the garrulous acrobat Batisto, whose speech is a
dazzling *mélange* of French, Italian, German, and Russian. The
story's wealth of semidocumentary material about circus life lends
it verisimilitude, while the details of wrestling technique in Chap-

ters II and V display Kuprin's expert knowledge of a sport that he sometimes refereed. In the Chekhov manner, the narrative is compressed, shorn of detail that would contribute little either to Arbuzov's spiritual condition or to the background against which it belongs.

Realism and humane concern lie at the heart of "At the Circus." Drawn from lived life and peopled with real types with whom Kuprin was closely familiar, it pointed the direction his best work would take in the years ahead.

III   "The Swamp"

Submitted first to *Russian Wealth,* "The Swamp" was rejected and appeared instead in the December issue of *God's World* for 1902. Though linked thematically with the Polesye cycle, it is set in the Zaraisk area of Ryazan Province, where Kuprin worked as a forest surveyor in late 1901. The tale has no plot; in Kuprin's words, it "consists entirely of mood."[15] Though its text is continuous, it falls into two distinct parts. The first is a philosophical prologue in which the student Serdyukov gives his views of the peasants and country life as he accompanies the surveyor Zhmakin through the forest at twilight. The second illustrates how mistaken his ideas are when both men spend the night in the keeper Stepan's hut, where they find parents and children the victims of malaria from the swamp around them.

The student confesses to Zhmakin that though he is not familiar with the country, all he has found in it so far is moving and beautiful. He marvels at the continuity of rural life. "A plough, a harrow, a hut, a cart.... Two thousand years ago these things were exactly the same as they are now" (III, 203). The native creativity of rural folk has produced what they require, but left no trace of the men who brought tools, customs, and beliefs into being. "Whatever you take," Serdyukov goes on, "clothing, utensils, bast shoes, a spade, a spinning wheel, a sieve! ... Generation after generation ... have racked their brains over the invention of these things ... and despite all this ... there's not a single name, not a single author!" (III, 203).

Serdyukov next speaks of the peasant's work on the land. Not only is he surrounded by the accumulated experience of his forefathers, but he also never doubts the usefulness of his toil. Unlike professional men, the peasant never need ask himself whether his labor is necessary to humanity: "For the peasant everything is amazingly orderly and clear. If you sow in spring then in winter you are fed. If you feed your horse it will feed you in return. What could be simpler or more certain?'' (III, 204). Thrust forcibly now by the march of time into the "civilized" world with its endless rules and regulations, the peasant is utterly mystified. Rejecting Zhmakin's views that the peasant is a stupid sluggard who should be beaten, the student explains that the *muzhik* (peasant) simply lives in a different dimension from more educated people. While they are already approaching the fourth dimension, he is only just beginning to grasp the third. But he is not at all stupid: "Just listen to him talking about the weather, his horse, or the haymaking . . . it's simple, apt, and expressive, and every word is weighed and fitting. . . .'' Carried away by his own words, Serdyukov concludes: "Yes, I know, the peasant's poor, ignorant, dirty. . . . Feed him, cure him, teach him to read and write, but don't crush him with your fourth dimension. . . . till you educate the people, all your Appeal Court decisions, compasses, notaries, and easements will be empty words of your fourth dimension to him!" (III, 206).

Kuprin handles the first half of "The Swamp" with great skill. Involved though they seem in the retelling, Serdyukov's ideas are essential to the impact made by the second half. The early pages rely for their effect on the contrast between the two men. The enthusiastic Serdyukov is set against the gloomy Zhmakin, who resents the voluble young man's presence and becomes painfully aware of his own old age under the student's barrage of words. Though Serdyukov does most of the talking and Zhmakin is essentially a sounding board, the author is careful to break up the student's tirade by frequent though brief exasperated retorts from the surveyor, so lending Serdyukov's words a more conversational flavor.

The second half of the tale brings an abrupt change of atmosphere. With the doleful boom of a bittern echoing in his ears, Serdyukov suddenly finds himself treading soft, slimy ground and surrounded by the clinging mist of a swamp. Meeting the keeper's family stricken with the fever that will eventually kill them all, the student is filled with despair. Unforgettable in its quiet horror, the "mood" to which Kuprin referred pervades the closing pages as remorselessly as the poisonous exhalations of the swamp seep into the hut. Sound is at the center of Kuprin's evocative technique here. A lonely island in a sea of mysterious stillness, the hut is filled with isolated but expressive sounds that intensify the silence of swirling mist outside: the plaintive humming of the samovar, the soporific chirping of a cricket, the monotonous creaking of the cradle, the fevered breathing of the sleeping children, and the mother's sad lullaby that seems to echo from the dawn of time when cavemen huddled round their fires. The sense of doom hanging over the family is heightened by Serdyukov's feeling that a "mysterious, invisible, bloodthirsty spirit" (III, 215) lurks like a curse in the hut, sucking its victims' lifeblood. The spirit of incurable disease is personified in a sinister picture called "Malaria" he saw long ago. In it a wild-eyed, ghostly woman rose with the mist from a swamp and slowly approached a child asleep at the water's edge.

Yet even in this wretched family there is beauty, all the more poignant for its transience. Looking at the face of Stepan's little girl, Serdyukov is struck by its sickly beauty: its features are so delicate that they seem "painted without shadow or color on translucent china," and its unusually large eyes are full of "naive astonishment, like the eyes of holy virgins in paintings by the pre-Raphaelites" (III, 211). Gazing at the lamp like one bewitched, her face is lit with a strangely expectant smile. Perhaps, Serdyukov muses, she longs for the night with its fever, when disease "takes possession of her little brain and wraps it in wild, tormentingly blissful dreams. . . " (III, 213).

Through Serdyukov, Kuprin reexamines his ideal of the "natural man" as portrayed in the Polesye cycle. The student is appalled by the quiet resignation with which Stepan regards his fate. Such instinctive submissiveness, Kuprin infers, is buried so deep in the peasant mentality that it is impossible to uproot. Stepan knows full well that he and his family are doomed: "We're all sick here. The wife and this child here and those on the stove. We buried the third on Tuesday. The place is damp. . . . We shiver and shiver . . . and then that's it!" (II, 211). When the student asks why he does not move elsewhere, Stepan replies: "If we don't live here then others will --- it's all the same where you live. Our father in heaven knows best where we should live and what we should do" (III, 211–12). Mystified by this simple-hearted man at peace with his life of poverty and disease, Serdyukov realizes that his earlier ideas were wrong. Bewildered, he asks himself how such suffering can possibly be justified. Neither he nor Kuprin provides an answer. To underline Stepan's submissiveness once more, the author has him called out in the dead of night to help fight a fire. Racked with fever, he goes obediently out into the mist that will eventually send him and his family to their graves. The precise significance of the story's finale is unclear. Waking at dawn, Serdyukov feels a sudden desire to see the sun. Crossing the swamp, he climbs above the mist and stops, filled with gladness, on top of a hill. Beneath him lies a shimmering sea of white mist, "but above him shone the blue sky... and the golden rays of the sun resounded with the jubilant triumph of victory" (III, 218). It is hard to agree with the Soviet critic F. I. Kuleshov's contention that the closing lines are a poetic expression of the joyous future for the downtrodden Stepans of Russia.[16] Though reminiscent of Chekhov's optimistic predictions, they seem to convey Serdyukov's relief at having left the swamp rather than any conviction of future social reform. His night in the hut has a dreamlike quality that his joy at the radiant morning helps him to escape. His feelings at the close have little connection with the plight of the peasant family. Like his author, and despite his theories, he offers no practical solution to Stepan's problem and that of millions like him.

Despite its equivocal ending, the symbolism of the tale is plain. Life for the peasant is a vast swamp whose poisonous miasmas of poverty and ignorance bring him suffering and death. But the advantages of civilization will not by themselves save him from destruction. As one critic put it in his review: "Here something bigger and wider is needed, something that embraces the whole of life ... in its comprehensiveness. Man is dying in the swamp, and *man* must be resurrected. And this task is more important and difficult than bread, medicine, and schooling..."[17] But Kuprin is content to show Stepan in death, not in resurrection. "The Swamp" remains a statement of the rural problem, not an answer to it.

IV   *The Underprivileged, the Downtrodden,*
and the Dispossessed

Other tales of these years focus not on the peasant but on the outcasts and *déclassés* of a society that measures success by wealth. In them we find people drawn from all sections of the lower classes. Actors and thieves, hobos and beggars, they are united by the poverty and squalor of their lives. Here again the breadth and depth of Kuprin's social experience emerge in the truth of his portrayal.

Set in a charity home for retired actors, "Na pokoe" ("In Retirement," 1902) reveals Kuprin's familiarity with the provincial Russian stage, a milieu he disliked intensely for its bickering and petty jealousies. Sustained by drink and the memory of past fame, the five inmates of the home live a useless life of boredom, enlivened only by arguments and vulgar talk of women. But Kuprin attenuates the grotesque vapidity of their existence with quiet tragedy. One of their number longs to see his granddaughter and is convinced she will visit him. But his pitiful dream remains unfulfilled, and during the stormy night of the closing lines he dies, alone and unloved.

Like his later tales "Zhidovka" ("The Jewess") and "Svad'ba" ("The Wedding"), "Trus" ("The Coward") of 1903 derives from Kuprin's observations during his army days of the life of poor Jewish communities on the Russo-Austrian border. The contrast between the tale's two main characters — the coarse smuggler Faibish and his reluctant partner in crime, the gentle Jewish actor Tsirelman — recalls that between the heroes of Gorky's "Chelkash" (1895). The likeness is no coincidence, for Gorky's tale impressed Kuprin. "I was struck," he recalled, "by the . . . exact description of the feelings of Chelkash and . . . the coward Gavrila. . . . I read this tale twice. . . ."[18]

The story is composed of two distinct episodes which could almost stand as independent tales. The second describes Faibish's lamentable smuggling expedition in which poverty compels Tsirelman to take part. Hesitant about his role and frightened by the darkness, he is seized with terror when the smuggler and he are fired on by a frontier guard, and screams in animal fear. If the second part of the tale is a gripping psychological study of a man in the clutches of terror, the first is a more subtle demonstration of the inspirational power of art. In a filthy tavern in the opening scene, Tsirelman acts out the traditional Jewish story of the rejection of an old man by his son. Against a backdrop of damp walls in a blue haze of tobacco smoke, he plays to an audience drinking cheap wine. They see the Tsirelman they all know miraculously transformed into an awesome figure of legend who thrills them with his sonorous words. Even in this incongruous setting, Kuprin affirms, art retains its power to move the hearts of men. Capable of stirring the most downtrodden of folk, Tsirelman's acting is extraordinarily talented, a quality thrown into bizarre relief by his cowardly behavior during the smuggling episode that follows.

The freedom-loving Faibish is akin to Buzyga, the hero of

"Konokrady" ("The Horse Thieves," 1903). But the horse thief
occupies the central position in that work, and is a more developed
character than his predecessor. Renowned for his resourcefulness,
he has become a notorious figure of country legend, one who despises the complacency of village life and prefers the exhilarating
existence of a thief on the run. Admiring this self-sufficient loner
who survives so skillfully beyond the pale of rural society, Kuprin
delights in the attractive fusion of opposites that makes Buzyga the
glamorous figure he is. In him, vengefulness coexists with kindness,
brutality with gentleness, and calculating evil with breathtaking
heroism. The fundamental nobility of his soul emerges in the
closing pages of the tale. Caught and horribly beaten by the infuriated villagers, he steadfastly refuses to betray his partners in
crime and so is torn to pieces by the crowd. Such outcasts on the
fringe of "respectable" society were not new in Kuprin's
work — his *Kiev Types* had presented a gallery of them. What is
new is the fierce determination with which Buzyga clings to his role
of pariah, considering it preferable to the accepted way of life
around him.

"Belyi pudel'" ("The White Poodle") is very different in tone
and content. Published in the journal *Yunyi chitatel' (The Young
Reader)* in 1904, it has become a favorite in Kuprin anthologies and
is one of his most popular works for the young. Set on the exotic
Crimean coast, it derives from Kuprin's acquaintance there with a
pair of wandering artists and their dog. In contrast to "The
Swamp" and "The Horse Thieves," it is an easy blend of lyricism
and gentle satire, spiced with a dash of adventure at the close and
rounded off by the happy ending typical of tales for younger
readers. Disarmingly simple as the work may seem, it effectively
illustrates the gulf separating the "haves" of Russian society from
the "have nots." The story pivots on the social contrast in its third
chapter between old Lodyzhkin and his young acrobat companion
Sergey on the one hand, and the rich family before whose dacha
they perform on the other. While Lodyzhkin and the boy have only
their beloved poodle Arto, the family are surrounded by all the
appurtenances of wealth. The artists are social outcasts whose only
link with respectable society consists in the coppers flung them for
their performance. Trilli, the spoilt son of the family, exhibits the
degeneracy resulting from the easy life. His infantile behavior sets
off the quiet maturity of Sergey as he calmly performs his acrobatic
tricks in the hope of a small reward. To Kuprin, the performers'
love of their art is a gauge of their spiritual beauty, a quality con-

firmed by their stubborn refusal to sell the poodle, whatever the price. They are the people whom Kuprin credits with nobility and goodness, people rejected as social nobodies by the wealthy to whom the rouble means all.

"The Jewess" (1904) strikes a more serious note. Published when pogroms against the Jews were regular occurrences in Russia, it demonstrates Kuprin's profound sympathy for this persecuted minority in Russian society. The tale is an eloquent reflection on the history and destiny of the Jewish race. Against his friends' advice, Kuprin chose to retain in his title the pejorative Russian term for Jew, *zhid,* instead of the neutral *evreika* (Jewess), and thus gave ironical emphasis to his pro-Jewish stance in the work.

Traveling on a winter's night to his post, the medical officer Kashintsev stops at a remote Jewish inn, where he is astounded by the incomparable beauty of the landlord's wife. The squalid poverty of the inn and the grubby slovenliness of the Jewess herself make her beauty more astonishing still — "He had not only never seen such radiant, proud, perfect beauty, but had not even dared think it might exist" (III, 343). The dazzling spectacle gives rise to an impassioned inner monologue in Kashintsev, which reveals Kuprin's own wonder at the Jewish race: "Amazing, inscrutable Jewish people! ... Through tens of centuries it has come,.. remaining fastidiously aloof from all other nations and concealing in its heart age-old grief and fire. The motley, vast life of Rome, Greece, and Egypt has long ago become the property of museum collections ... but this mysterious people ... has preserved ... its faith,.. the sacred language of its inspired, divine books,.. and its mystical alphabet whose very outlines are pervaded by thousand year old antiquity! ... versatile and immortal, it lives on, as if in fulfillment of some supernatural predestination. Its whole history is ... drenched with its own blood: centuries-old captivity, coercion, hatred, servitude, torment, bonfires of human flesh, exile, dispossession.... How has it remained alive?" (III, 347–48).

In the divine beauty of the woman's face, the doctor sees proof of the immortality of the Jewish people. How many millennia, he wonders, must her race have stood apart from others to preserve these exquisite biblical features that hark back to Judith, Ruth, and Rachel? Lost in a distant corner of the Jewish Pale, the woman is the embodiment of some miracle, and before her Kashintsev senses his own insignificance. "What am I," he muses, "yesterday's savage and today's intellectual,.. beside this living enigma, perhaps the greatest and most inexplicable enigma in the history of mankind?" (III, 349).

Though cut short by the appearance of a vulgar local policeman, Kashintsev's reverie casts a shadow of poignant sadness over his life. Like that of Stepan's daughter in "The Swamp," the beauty of the Jewess comes as a profoundly moving surprise, a blinding anomaly in an environment of penury and degradation. Kuprin's point is that not even the foul mire at the lowest depths of man's existence can destroy the essential beauty of certain human beings. Yet Kashintsev's experience has a curiously insubstantial quality. So exceptional is it that like the night spent by Serdyukov in "The Swamp," it acquires the ephemerality of a dream. As the doctor drives away into the winter darkness, all that remains of the woman's beauty is a bright but wistful memory, flickering like the light of a station left far behind.

If tales like "The Jewess" and "The Swamp" show human beings condemned by circumstance to remain in the low social stratum into which they are born, then "Off the Street" (1904) describes a man of comparatively high social standing who has sunk to the nadir of degeneration. Andrey, the "man off the street" whose life story constitutes the whole of the work, is probably based on P. D. Manych,[19] a minor literary figure in Petersburg and one of Kuprin's boon companions renowned for his chequered past. The peculiar staccato delivery of his speech, with its frequent questions and exclamations, provides the driving force behind Andrey's narrative.

His account of how he became a *déclassé* echoes the confessions of Dostoevskian characters tormented by the unstable amalgam of base and noble impulses within them. Though he describes himself as "a striking example of moral and physical degeneration resulting from hereditary alcoholism, poor food, exhaustion, and venereal disease" (III, 364), he is also sensitive, intelligent, and highly versatile. His decline is the result of environmental factors rather than of fecklessness or irresponsibility. A home background of beatings, drunkenness, and adultery was followed by a succession of schools from which he was expelled. Next came the army, with its drinking and gambling, a sordid affair with another officer's wife, and dismissal for cheating at cards. Jobs as varied as Kuprin's own were followed by work on a provincial paper, where "there was no need to have any talent or the ability to read and write" (III, 375). Dismissed again, he was forced to become a professional beggar (*strelok*) and then a waiter. Arrested for his part in the murder of a hotel guest, he was acquitted and released after six months in an asylum. Showing the demoralizing effect on his hero of every stage in his life, Kuprin points the finger of accusation at the traditional pillars of "respectable" society — the family, the school, and the army — and shows that beneath their façade all are equally corrupt. Unable to offer Andrey scope to apply his talents effectively, society's only recourse now it has made him a hobo is to fling him out on the street. Society, Kuprin infers, not Andrey, is the loser.

As "Off the Street" shows, destructive social forces are at their most concentrated in the urban environment. In the tale "Chernyi tuman" ("Black Fog," 1905), those forces are allegorically represented in the poisonous emanation of the city that seeps into body and soul and brings with it death. Boris, the Little Russian hero of the tale, comes north to Petersburg to make his fortune, but instead falls victim to consumption. The familiar product of that city's climate, the disease becomes for Boris the malevolent distillation of everything evil in this dark, inhospitable metropolis so alien to his beloved south. Consumption lurks in the city's gloom like a predatory snake, its fetid breath a loathsome blend of "the sins of men, their malice and hatred, the exhalations of their mattresses, the odor of sweat and putrid mouths" (III, 406). Said by Kuprin to be written of himself, "Black Fog" reveals his antipathy to "flabby, cold, pale, boring Petersburg" (III, 400) and her grey people with no sunlight in their souls.

V *Hypocrites, Bigots, and Degenerates*

Not content with showing the plight of the poor and dispossessed of Russian society, Kuprin also exposed the hypocrisy of "respectable" people whose reactionary attitudes made that society what it was. One such is Nasedkin, the retired school teacher of "Mirnoe zhitie" ("A Quiet Life," 1904), Kuprin's first work to appear in a *Knowledge* miscellany. Nasedkin (his name derives from the Russian *nasedka,* a sitting hen) is a self-appointed guardian of social order who writes anonymous letters denouncing inhabitants of his town in the belief that he is doing good. In his blind respect for authority he is the spiritual brother of Belikov, the classics teacher of Chekhov's tale "Man in a Case" (1898), whose encapsulated life shields him from reality. Nasedkin's thirty-five years as a pedagogue have taught him to be constantly watchful. Just as earlier he

committed the results of his observations of his pupils to a note-
book, so now he secretly records the names and circumstances of
the victims of his anonymous letters — "all the scandals, love intrigues, gossip, and rumor of this sleepy little philistine town"
(III, 302).

The withering power of this laconic satire derives from the glaring contrast in Nasedkin between appearance and reality, how he
seems to himself and others, and how he really is. Outwardly he is a
model gentleman enjoying a quiet retirement. Everything in his
little apartment — from its tulle curtains and pink lampshade to its
old-fashioned repp furniture and corner icon — suggests peaceful
respectability. In the stillness of his room, pervaded by the smell of
geraniums, Nasedkin reflects with pride on "his honorable old age,
serene, neat, and respected by all" (III, 300), his full pension, and
his thousands carefully salted away over the years.

If Nasedkin is genuinely unaware of the harm his letters cause,
Kuprin is not. In the latter half of the tale, when Nasedkin goes
devoutly to church, Kuprin shows the depth of his hypocrisy and
the suffering his letters bring. By cleverly weaving Nasedkin's
thoughts into the background of the service, Kuprin reveals with
biting irony Nasedkin's view of himself as an arm of the law: ". . . I
add my drop of benefit to the common good: I caution and warn
those who require it, open their eyes and set them on the right
road" (III, 308). When a tall woman in black enters the church,
Nasedkin recognizes Shcherbacheva, the wife of a bestial millionaire merchant forty years her senior. Warned by a letter from
Nasedkin, he caught her one day with his bailiff, had her stripped
in front of the servants, and flogged her savagely. Her spirit
broken, the young woman is now a virtual recluse. Watching her
sobbing on her knees as the priest intones a prayer for fornica-
tresses, Nasedkin gloats over his success in setting her on the path
of righteousness. Convinced that his own life is free from sin, he
believes proudly that his zeal in unmasking transgression assures
him a special place in the life to come. To Kuprin the church and its
traditional conservatism foster the activities of people like Nasedkin, who impose their own standards on others. The bigotry of
Nasedkin and the dogma of the church complement each other in a
society riddled with prejudice and hypocrisy.

While "A Quiet Life" contains no positive character as a mouthpiece for Kuprin's views, three other tales of the early 1900s turn on
conflict between members of respectable society and progressive

representatives of the intelligentsia, in whom the author's voice is heard. The first and best is the Crimean story "Kor' " ("Measles," 1904). Socially and materially, its protagonists are diametrically opposed: the wealthy shipowner Zavalishin and the impecunious student Voskresensky, tutor to his children. The student is an intelligent young man of democratic views, while his employer is the embodiment of rabid Russian chauvinism. Everything about Zavalishin is extravagantly Russian: his house furnished in ungainly, pseudo-Russian style; his fantastic dress of silk Russian blouse and high patent leather boots; and his beard *à la mouzhik*. The result is an absurd caricature, reminiscent of the provincial impresario strutting in fake Russian costume.

But Zavalishin's attitudes are even more offensive than his affectation, and it is they that bring about the confrontation with Voskresensky in the second part of the tale. Convinced of the superiority of the Russian nation over all others, Zavalishin is infuriated by foreign exploitation of his country's resources. As he attacks the Jews, his abusive words reveal in him the vicious anti-Semitism of the reactionary Black Hundred movement of the early 1900s. Too long suppressed, the student's indignation bursts forth in an impassioned tirade against his hateful opponent: "Your ideal, all-Russian fist that squeezes the blood out of the little minority people you despise, isn't dangerous to anyone. It's just purely and simply loathsome, like every symbol of force. You're not a disease, not a sore, you're just an inevitable, tiresome rash, like measles" (III, 324). His anger rising, Voskresensky denounces the falsity of Zavalishin's pose, based as it is on popular but erroneous notions of the Russian people. Masking the poverty and suffering of the people it purports to epitomize, Zavalishin's affectation of all things Russian is only an "absurd masquerade" of life *à la russe* with a "moiré silk lining" (III, 325).

More outspoken than those of his predecessors Bobrov (*Moloch*) and Pchelovodov ("A Muddle"), Voskresensky's protest hits the mark, and though immediately dismissed by his employer, he emerges the moral victor. His confrontation with Zavalishin exemplifies the wider conflict between progressive and reactionary Russia. Kuprin's optimism as to the eventual outcome of that struggle is subtly displayed by the story's close. Though tinged with regret, the loathing Voskresensky feels for Zavalishin's wife after she has seduced him on the eve of his departure underlines his total rejection of the family and its values.

Like "Measles," the shorter tale "Khoroshee obshchestvo" ("Good Company," 1905) shows a collision of opposite types leading to a rupture between them, but it lacks the power of its predecessor. The work shows signs of hasty composition, probably to be explained by the fact that at the time of writing (spring, 1905), Kuprin was hurrying to finish *The Duel*. The tale's protagonist, the young writer Druzhinin, feels like a poor relative in the rich Bashkirtsev household, where he is considered an undesirable suitor for Rita, the daughter of the family. The father's reluctance to help a friend of Rita's because it might damage his reputation leads to a fierce argument between Bashkirtsev and Druzhinin that reveals their long-concealed antipathy. To Bashkirtsev's remark that the young man's company is harmful to his daughter, Druzhinin retorts in fury: "the most harmful, corrupting, filthy company for your daughter is your own, your shady operations . . . your lack of principles . . . and humanity, — that's what will corrupt her, not my company" (III, 423). Once again, the moral victory rests with Kuprin's intellectual hero, and though Bashkirtsev attempts a reconciliation, Druzhinin breaks with the family for good.

If "Good Company" is Kuprin's indictment of the speculator who hides his machinations beneath a veneer of respectability, "Zhrets" ("The High Priest," 1905) is a more fundamental criticism of the monied society to which Bashkirtsev belongs. Through the eyes of its physician hero Chudinov, it lays bare the moral and physical degeneration of the idle rich. Though it contains no verbal conflict of the kind pivotal to "Measles" and "Good Company," the tale sets its democratically inclined hero in a horrifying setting of hereditary disease and bodily corruption. Called to a wealthy household to attend a dying paralytic, Chudinov discovers that the man's son is an imbecile and that his daughter's fiancé is suffering from venereal disease. Thus the whole line is tainted, from father through son to children-to-be, with an ineradicable infection symbolizing the degeneracy of their class. Appalled by the spectacle, Chudinov looks back on a career devoted to the treatment of such people and recognizes its tragic pointlessness: "Why do I soil myself with these sickly people, my patients? So they can bring idiots into the world like the one we've just seen?" (III, 436).

VI *Philosophical Miniatures*

Beside the realism of his other tales of the early 1900s, Kuprin's four philosophical miniatures of 1904 strike a dissonant note. Each touches on the mysterious forces of destiny that rule men's lives, and in their somber settings of evening and night, they echo such earlier works as "In the Dark."

"Bril'ianty" ("The Diamonds") examines the effect on passers-by of two large gems in a shop window. On every face gazing at their rainbow brilliance can be read the secret longing to possess the stones. "Who knows," Kuprin asks, "what would be found in the best human souls if one could only . . . observe their most secret, hidden corners? How many . . . honest citizens would prove to be thieves, murderers, and adulterers?" (III, 356). Absurdly, man has made these fragments of condensed carbon the quintessential symbol of wealth and honor. But above all they signify power, power that down the ages has brought war and death in its train. "Pustye dachi" ("Empty Dachas") is a more delicate piece, full of the author's nostalgia for the past. As autumn sets in with her late flowers and cold sky, the narrator senses that the summer of his life is gone forever. The happiness of bygone years is as irrevocable as the radiantly beautiful girl who once skipped enchantingly past him and out of his life. The inexorable passage of time is embodied for him in the obscure but menacing creature, "vast, unseen, omniscient and cruel" (III, 358), that lies silently beyond the hills and smiles at the autumn with malevolent joy. "Belye nochi" ("White Nights") offers a somber picture of the mystical Petersburg night, evoked in the author by the very different, luxuriantly festive nights of the Crimea. Walking the streets of the sleeping city, he visualizes the hundreds of people asleep in its vast buildings, so strangely close yet so far from one another. The time will come, he reflects, when the last human beings will die, but Petersburg's massive, mute buildings will outlive them all, staring into the silent void with their blind, dead eyes.

"Vechernii gost' " ("An Evening Guest") is the longest and most sinister of the miniatures. Here the cruel creature of "Empty Dachas" is fate itself, which holds us all in its unfathomable power. A knock on his door at evening triggers in the narrator thoughts about the horrifyingly chance quality of all our lives. Life is an awesome lottery: "I do not know what will happen to me to-morrow . . . in an hour, in a minute; I live like a gambler for whom fate spins a wheel full of surprises" (III, 295). Only one thing is sure in this game of hazard on the brink of the abyss — death, that most chance yet most certain of guests. In the stillness of his room the narrator wonders fearfully whether the sudden visitor outside his door is destiny himself, come to claim his ineluctable due.

Imbued with the fashionable pessimism of the Decadent movement, the miniatures are anomalous pieces amid Kuprin's work of the early 1900s, in which realism and social concern are paramount. His tales of these years display an increasing awareness of the injustice that bedevils a society so rigidly divided into rich and poor, a schism that was reinforced by the powerful apparatus of autocratic control. Fundamental to that control was the Russian military machine so virulently denounced by Kuprin's most famous work, *The Duel*.

CHAPTER 4

The Duel

I *Genesis*

THE writing of *The Duel* took well over a decade and was a
laborious process. Kuprin first conceived it in his second year
in the army, when he thought of writing a story to reveal the "horror and tedium of army life."[1] After embarking on the work, he
was dissatisfied with his first drafts and destroyed them. Not until
1902 did he return to the project, fired by his anger at an incident in
a Petersburg restaurant when a group of drunken officers insulted
his wife. "Sooner or later," he told her, "I'll write about our
'valorous' army — our pitiful, downtrodden soldiers and our
ignorant officers wallowing in drunkenness."[2]

The years since the publication of "The Enquiry" had seen a
series of army tales by Kuprin, among them "A Night's Lodging"
(1895), "Nochnaia smena" ("Night Relief," 1899), and "The
March" (1901), all of which served as preliminary sketches for the
detailed portrayal of military life in *The Duel*. More important was
"V kazarme" ("In the Barracks"), published in 1903 and later
incorporated into Chapter XI of the novel. Many of its characters
appeared in *The Duel:* for example, its shy, young lieutenant Zybin
is the prototype of Romashov.

Linked closely as it was with Kuprin's own army days, the creation of his novel was an intensely cathartic experience, as his words
to his wife reveal: "The main character is myself. . . . I must free
myself from the heavy burden of impressions accumulated by my
years of military service. I will call this novel *The Duel,* because it
will be my duel . . . with the tsarist army. The army cripples the
soul, destroys all a man's finest impulses, and debases human dignity. . . . With all the strength of my soul I hate . . . my years of
regimental service. I must write about all I have known and seen.

And with my novel I shall challenge the tsarist army to a duel."[3]

But the work went slowly, chiefly because his duties for *God's World* left him little time for anything else. He had difficulty, too, finding a suitable surname for his hero, one that would imprint itself on the reader's mind without being too outlandish. The question was vitally important to him: "My hero is myself. Into him I put my own dreams, secret feelings, and thoughts. I must love him and believe in him as I believe in myself."[4] Early in 1903 Kuprin accidentally hit on the memorable name Romashov, that of a Nizhny Novgorod magistrate whom his wife mentioned in conversation. He wrote the first six chapters in Miskhor, near Yalta, but was so dismayed by the similarity between Nazansky's views in Chapter V and those of Vershinin in Chekhov's *Three Sisters* that he tore up the manuscript. Fortunately, his wife managed to glue the sixty pages together again. In the spring of 1904 — after his resignation from *God's World* — Kuprin returned to the novel, and by August was working on it intensively. Now he realized that *The Duel* would be the most momentous work of his career, and in a letter to Batyushkov wrote that it was his "ninth wave," his "final examination."[5]

Despite his enthusiasm, Kuprin fell far behind schedule. In his efforts to finish *The Duel* during the winter of 1904–1905, he even took a separate room in the capital and was only allowed by his wife to visit her when he had produced fresh chapters. Nor was the situation improved when in January the police confiscated Chapter XIV during a raid on his lodgings in Sergiev Posad (now Zagorsk), ninety versts from Moscow, where he had gone to work in peace and quiet.[6] (He later rewrote the chapter from memory.) Pressed by *Knowledge* to submit his manuscript no later than Easter of 1905, he found the closing chapter exceedingly troublesome. Written only hours before the deadline, it described the duel between Romashov and Nikolaev, but Kuprin felt dissatisfied with his conclusion and tore it up. He replaced it with the hastily written one page official report of the duel that now ends the work.

Kuprin's debt to Gorky for his help in writing the novel was immense, as he later readily acknowledged: "Gorky was a compassionate colleague . . . and knew how to give support and encouragement at the right time. I remember I abandoned *The Duel* many times . . . , but after reading the chapters I had written Gorky went into raptures over them and even shed a few tears. If he had not inspired me with confidence . . . I might not have finished my novel."[7] On the eve of the novel's publication Kuprin wrote to Gorky: "Now that all is finished at last, I can say that everything bold and turbulent in my tale belongs to you. If only you knew how much I have learnt from you and how grateful I am to you for it."[8] When *The Duel* finally appeared on May 3, 1905, in Volume Six of the *Knowledge* miscellanies, it bore the dedication: "To Maxim Gorky with sincere friendship and profound respect."[9]

The Duel promptly became the literary sensation of the year. The twenty thousand copies of the miscellany were rapidly sold out, necessitating a second printing within a month, with the result that in 1905 alone some forty thousand five hundred copies were sold — a vast number for the early 1900s. After the arduous years of fitful writing when he had despaired of ever finishing the novel, Kuprin suddenly found himself the cynosure of every eye.

* * * *

The Duel tells of its hero's growing distaste for army life and his gradual realization that he is a uniquely individual human being. But before he is able to leave the army to act on that realization, he is killed in a duel by the husband of the woman he loves.

II   *The Opening Chapter*

The first chapter of *The Duel* is a prologue designed to outline many issues central to the work as a whole. Furthermore, it offers a glimpse of the hero's position vis-à-vis army life and its traditional preoccupations, dwelling in particular on his attitude to injustice and violence. Though in early pages of the chapter Kuprin makes no attempt to single out his hero, by the close the course of events has moved Romashov into the forefront of the action, and we have little doubt about his central role in the novel.

With his very first sentence Kuprin plunges us into the thick of army life, as the evening exercises in guard duty draw to a close. The dismal generality of the scene is reinforced by a deliberate neglect of locational detail. Kuprin makes only the most perfunctory references to the setting: a row of poplars bordering the road and the parade ground itself. Amid these colorless surroundings the noncommissioned officers test their sentries' knowledge of regulations by attempting to distract them, or to trick them into surrendering their rifles. Kuprin provides a glimpse of two soldiers obliged to undergo these tedious exercises, both of whom are scorned by their officers. The first is Khlebnikov, destined to play an essential role in the novel as the epitome of the persecuted common Russian soldier. Here his slowness at learning the sentry's routine brings angry abuse from his corporal, Shapovalenko. The second, the Tatar Mukhamedzhinov, is shown in more detail. He can barely understand Russian, and is totally perplexed by the efforts to confuse him in drill. Wild-eyed and frightened, he suddenly loses his temper and threatens to bayonet anyone who comes near.

After the men, Kuprin examines the officers in more detail. He sketches their appearance or temperament in swift, broad strokes, dwelling on characteristics that particularize them throughout the novel. Lance Corporal Shapovalenko is a small, round man who shouts at his men; the company commander, Captain Sliva, is hunched, with an ambling gait; Lieutenant Vetkin is described as "a bald, moustached man of about thirty-three, a convivial, garrulous fellow, a songster and drunkard" (IV, 8); and Ensign Lbov is "a lively, well-built lad with ... a perpetual smile on his thick, naive lips." Of the three junior officers mentioned, Romashov is accorded least attention. Kuprin writes of his hero at this stage merely that "he was only in his second year in the regiment," slipping these words between the more amplified references to his fellows Vetkin and Lbov. As yet we have no notion of Romashov's appearance or character, and he says almost nothing as the officers converse. Instead it is Vetkin who expresses his annoyance that the exercises have no yet ended and adds that the whole performance is pointless anyway. The common soldier is always pushed too hard before an inspection, he says, with the result that he becomes stupefied by it all.

Not content with describing those present, Kuprin offers through their conversation glimpses of other officers who are for the moment off stage but will later join in the drama. Thus passing references reveal Lieutenant Andrusevich, who makes his company sing in chorus in the evening; Lieutenant Colonel Lekh, who is found drunk in the officers' club; and Colonel Shulgovich, who roars at his officers in front of orderlies.

The arrival on horseback of the dashing aide Bek-Agamalov injects vigor into this first summary picture of the officers and triggers the emergence of Romashov as an individualized character. At the sight of Bek riding his golden horse the consummate skill, Romashov utters words of rapturous admiration. A romanitc, exotic figure, Bek is a thoroughbred Circassian, "lean wiry, and very strong" (IV, 9). Together with physical power, his appearance suggests a malign streak in his nature that emerges later on: "With its sloping forehead, slender, hooked nose and resolute, firm lips, his face ... had not yet lost its characteristic oriental pallor...."

When Bek volunteers the information that the colonel has ordered sabre practice for all officers, the conversation turns to violence and the defense of military honor. It is now that *The Duel* acquires the driving force that will propel its hero to growing self-awareness, and eventually hurl him to his death. When Vetkin questions the usefulness of the sabre in modern warfare, Bek asks what he would do if he were insulted by some civilian. The question and the conversation it produces indicate the contempt shown by Russian officers for civilians at the time. Such contempt often manifested itself in acts of violence committed ostensibly to defend "the honor of their uniform." When Lbov recalls a lieutenant who shot a barman for pulling his shoulder strap, the group take up a familiar topic of conversation — "instances of sudden, bloody, on-the-spot reckonings, and of how these incidents almost always went unpunished" (IV, 12). Examples follow thick and fast: the drunken cornet who hacked his way through a crowd of Jews in a small town; the lieutenant who slashed a student to death in a Kiev dance hall for jogging his elbow; and the officer in a Moscow or Peters-burg restaurant who shot a civilian "like a dog" for his remark that respectable men do not pester ladies with whom they are unacquainted.

The examples prompt Romashov to make his first comment of the conversation. Blushing with embarrassment, coughing and adjusting his glasses in his nervousness, he protests hesitantly: "Look gentlemen, this is what I say.... A barman ... if he's a civilian ... a respectable man, someone from the gentry and so on ... why should I attack him with a sabre when he's unarmed? Why can't I demand satisfaction from him? After all, we're civilized people, so to speak..." (IV, 13). Though mild, Romashov's words illustrate a fundamental difference between him and his fellows on the issue of military honor, a difference reinforced by Vetkin's retort: "Eh, you're talking rubbish, Romashov." The scene of sabre practice that follows heightens the difference by revealing Romashov's incompetence with the sword, a failing that symbol-izes his organic unsuitability for a way of life committed to vio-lence. In a single sentence aside as his hero draws his sabre and con-fusedly adjusts his glasses (that traditional hallmark of the intellec-tual), Kuprin describes Romashov as "of medium height, thin, and

... quite strong for his build" (IV, 14), though his great shyness makes him clumsy. Never good with a sword even at the Academy, after eighteen months in the army he has forgotten how to use one. As he strikes at the clay dummy his left arm gets in the way and the falling blade grazes his index finger, drawing blood. This first, minor injury prefigures both his spiritual pain and his physical death in the novel.

If Romashov's clumsiness with the sabre indicates his unsuitability for the army, Bek's terrifying skill with the weapon exemplifies the violence of military life. Demonstrating how the power of the sword stroke should come not from the arm but the wrist, he emphasizes the downward sawing action that makes the blow more terrible. Holding his left arm behind his back, he strikes the dummy faster than the eye can see: "Romashov heard only the shrill whistle of the blade ... and immediately the upper half of the dummy slumped softly and heavily to the ground. The surface of the cut was just as smooth as if it had been polished" (IV, 15). For an instant the sabre slash reveals Bek's cruelly rapacious nature: "He was breathing heavily, and ... the whole of him, with his malicious, staring eyes, his hooked nose and bared teeth, resembled some proud, evil bird of prey."

The appearance of Colonel Shulgovich, the regimental commander, brings Romashov closer to the center of the stage. Shulgovich is a foul-mouthed old officer who terrifies the ranks, hypnotizing the men with his severe, pale eyes. When the Tatar Sharafutdinov fails to understand a question the colonel puts to him, Shulgovich swears volubly at him and orders him to stand guard in full kit as punishment. His heart hammering at this injustice, Romashov intercedes for the soldier, explaining that he understands no Russian. In a rage, Shulgovich sentences Romashov to four days' house arrest for insubordination. Once again the hero is at odds with his milieu, this time not through martial ineptitude but through sensitivity to injustice. His temperamental dissimilarity from his fellow officers is underlined by their jibes at his lack of manliness: Bek contemptuously calls him a "schoolgirl" as he bandages his bleeding finger, and Captain Sliva tells him he should be at his mother's breast instead of in the army.

In this chapter Kuprin reveals progressively more about his hero by distinguishing him from the army system of which he is part. Its closing lines take the process further by demonstrating the hero's sensitivity once again: despite his bitterness at Sliva's cutting words, Romashov pities him, "this lonely, coarse, unloved man who had only two interests in all the world: the beautiful drill of his company and his quiet, solitary, daily drinking" (IV, 18). But Kuprin modifies his closing lines with a gently mocking thrust aimed as much at the melodramatic excesses of his own early tales as at his hero. As Romashov watches Sliva trudge away, Kuprin notes his "rather ridiculous, naive habit" — common to the very young — of "thinking of himself in the third person in the words of hackneyed novels." The present situation produces the appropriate words, as he thinks inwardly of himself: "His kind, expressive eyes were clouded by sadness." Indicative of his romantic notions, Romashov's imaginative habit affirms the abyss separating his ideals from the reality around him. By the close of *The Duel* that abyss yawns immeasurably wide and into it Romashov plunges to his doom.

III *The Officer Caste*

Though set a decade before 1905, *The Duel* was interpreted as an oblique commentary on events in the Far East at the time. Its appearance in May 1905 could hardly have been more opportune, bracketed as it was by the echoes of two Russian defeats at the hands of the Japanese: the fall of Port Arthur in January, and the annihilation of the Baltic Fleet at Tsushima in May. Amid national ignominy, *The Duel* seemed a revelation of the reasons for Russia's defeat in the Far East. The responsibility for that defeat, it implied, lay squarely on the shoulders of Russian officers in the field, and events on the Pacific had demonstrated to all the inefficiency and corruption of the Russian military machine. "The officers," wrote Lenin, "proved uneducated, backward and unprepared, lacking close ties with their soldiers and not enjoying their confidence."[10] In the general assault on Russian autocracy mounted in 1905, the officer caste became the target for particular attack.[11]

While his predecessors Leo Tolstoy and Vsevolod Garshin had shown the army in combat situations, Kuprin portrays it in peacetime, so underlining the brutality of military life as a whole. His gallery of officer types, some thirty in all, reveals in the microcosm of one regiment the attitudes that make the Russian army the crassly degenerate body it is. Kuprin draws the majority of his officers with light irony, sharp mockery, or outright contempt. To those glimpsed in the opening scene are added Lieutenant Nikolaev, husband of Shurochka with whom Romashov is in love, an oxlike man stubbornly making his third attempt at the examinations for the General Staff Academy; Captain Leshchenko, a silent figure with the drooping face of a melancholy bloodhound; the regimental card sharper Lieutenant Archakovsky, a man of doubtful character said to have once killed a coachman with his fists; the blasé Lieutenant Bobetinsky, who at twenty-four affects a languorous disillusionment and sprinkles his speech with bad French; little Captain Svetovidov, who steals his soldiers' money to buy drink; the huge, awesome Captain Osadchy; Olizar, a lean, carefully groomed aide with a foppish, wrinkled face; and the adjutant Fedorovsky, cold-eyed, haughty, and strictly correct.

Of this catalogue of officers, Osadchy deserves special mention as the dread incarnation of military violence. Renowned for his powerful voice, his enormous size and terrible strength, he can subjugate the most undisciplined troops. In Osadchy's pale face, framed by hair so dark it is almost blue, Romashov senses "something tense, cruel . . . characteristic not of a man but of a huge, powerful wild beast" (IV, 85). But not until the picnic scene in Chapter XIV does his bloodthirsty atavism emerge in all its horror. When the guests begin to argue about the impending war with Germany, the drunken Osadchy speaks with nostalgia of olden days when war was war, bloody, merciless, and cruel: "War has degenerated . . . the days of real, savage, merciless war have gone. . . . In the Middle Ages they know how to fight all right. . . . a city is stormed by night. The whole of it set ablaze. . . . The bottoms of wine barrels knocked out. Blood and wine running in the streets. . . . Women — naked, beautiful, weeping — dragged along by the hair. There was no pity for them. They were the sweet booty of the brave! . . . At night the houses burned, the wind blew, and black bodies swung on the gallows, while above them the ravens cried. And under the gallows the bonfires burned and the victors feasted. There were no prisoners. Why take them? . . . What a courageous, wonderful time! What people those were! . . . I drink to the joy of former wars, to merry, bloody cruelty!" (IV, 131). Osadchy's words evoke a sympathetic response in Bek, his spiritual brother. Seeking an outlet for the ancestral barbarism roused in him by Osadchy's tirade, he draws his sabre and slashes savagely at a sapling nearby. The brutality of Osadchy, Kuprin infers, is common in varying degrees to all his fellows.

But not all the officers incur Kuprin's censure; a handful of them are portrayed with sympathy as embodying qualities that distinguish them from their unsavory fellows. The most interesting is Second Lieutenant Mikhin, a small, timid man whom Romashov likes. An episodic figure, he is the only officer who resembles the hero in temperament. We first glimpse Mikhin in the officers' club in Chapter VIII when he expresses views on dueling akin to the hero's. He next appears as the guests leave for the picnic in Chapter XIII, when he asks Romashov to sit beside his sisters to prevent the cynical Dits from upsetting them with his suggestive talk. The picnic reveals an unexpected side to Mikhin: in his wrestling bout with Olizar he astonishes everyone by throwing his bigger opponent twice, a symbolic triumph of the humane over the brutal. Significantly, Mikhin is the only officer to express sympathy for Romashov when he is summoned before the tribunal toward the end of the novel: ". . . with tears in his eyes he shook his [Romashov's] hand hard . . . blushed, hastily and awkwardly put on his coat, and left" (IV, 193).

Three other peripheral characters enjoy Kuprin's sympathy though they are given less space than Mikhin: the Corps Commander who reviews the regiment at the May parade (Chapter XV); Captain Stelkovsky, who commands the Fifth Company; and Lieutenant Colonel Rafalsky, commander of the Fourth Battalion. The anonymous Corps Commander is modeled on General Dragomirov, commander of the Kiev Military District during Kuprin's army years, a soldier renowned for his opposition to rigid Prussian techniques of military training. Through him Kuprin condemns the officers for their lack of concern for the ranks, that "most sacred, grey soldiery" (IV, 149) that readily gives its life for its officers in battle. Stelkovsky's quiet skill in drilling his company makes him an exception "perhaps unique in the whole Russian army" (IV, 143). Avoiding brutality, with patience he achieves in a day results that take others a week. Consequently, his men are the elite of the regiment, superbly drilled and devoted to their commander. Rafalsky is very different. An eccentric, solitary bachelor who rarely mixes with his fellow officers, he lavishes his affection on the many creatures he keeps in his quarters. His kindness to the denizens of his menagerie is paralleled by the generosity with which he lends money to younger colleagues. Yet for all his admiration of their unusual qualities, Kuprin shows that there are darker sides to both Stelkovsky and Rafalsky: the latter beats his men just like any other officer, and Stelkovsky is a secret debauchee who seduces underage peasant girls. Desperate tedium hangs over army life like a suffocating pall and makes Kuprin's officers what they are. All are in the service only because they are unfit for any other occupation. There are a few careerists, but the vast majority regard their duties as "a compulsory, annoying, and loathsome *corvée*" (IV, 56). While the younger officers do the minimum required, the company commanders are embroiled in family squabbles, live above their means, and contract debts. At the insistence of their wives, many "borrow" from company funds or withhold money enclosed with soldiers' letters. Several of them only survive by gambling, much of it dishonest. All drink heavily, either in the club, in each other's quarters, or, like Sliva, in melancholy solitude, a daily routine broken only by an occasional argument or a group sortie to the local brothel. Regimental life is a desert of perpetual intellectual aridity. Most of the officers have forgotten how to think, still less how to state their views on fundamental issues. The attitude toward intellectual activity in the army is summed up by Vetkin's response to Romashov's despair at the pointlessness of military life: "...if you think like that, it'd be better not to be in the army ... in our job it doesn't do to think" (IV, 111). The cultural wilderness of army life is nicely pointed up by the symbolic treatment accorded Romashov's plaster bust of Pushkin. While his illiterate orderly Gainan, a pagan Cheremis, worships it as a god, the drunken officer Vetkin sees in it only some despicable civilian and uses it for target practice. In revealing Vetkin's crass ignorance, the ironic episode inverts the traditional roles of officer and orderly, and symbolizes what Kuleshov calls "the duel between barbarity and civilization"[12] at the heart of *The Duel*. Only two days later, Romashov uses Vetkin's revolver in his duel with Nikolaev, who embodies for the hero much that he finds loathsome in the officer caste.

If tedium and sterility are the pervasive essence of army life, then violence is the inevitable result of the frustration they bring. Might is right in this world of the fist, and the officers rule their men by as much brutality as is necessary to reduce the common soldier to a petrified animal. Physical force and the verbal abuse that accompanies it are a relentless refrain through *The Duel* and become the most repulsive distinguishing mark of the officer type. Violence reaches its apogee during preparations for the May parade, as the ranks are drilled mercilessly hour after hour in the intense heat: "On all sides, from every company and platoon came the continuous sound of men being slapped in the face. Often from a distance ... Romashov would see some infuriated company commander start to hit all his soldiers across the face in turn, from the left to the right flank. First the soundless sweep of the hand and then ... the dry crack of the blow, and again, and again, and again.... The noncoms beat their men cruelly for a trivial mistake — beat them till the blood flowed, knocked out their teeth, smashed their eardrums ... knocked them to the ground.... It never occurred to anyone to complain: they were in the grip of some general, monstrous, sinister nightmare; some absurd hypnosis had taken possession of the regiment" (IV, 142). Its senseless violence was what sickened Kuprin most about army life. The spectre of sanctioned brutality stalks the pages of *The Duel* from beginning to end as Kuprin writes out his pain and horror. Romashov's growing loathing for the violence he sees daily around him accelerates his alienation from the officer caste.

IV *Duels and Dueling*

Dueling is a formal manifestation of military violence, and references to it are frequent throughout the novel. Indeed the subject of duels was a topical one in the 1890s. May 1894 saw the introduction of "Rules for the investigation of quarrels amongst officers," regulations that authorized dueling when a duel was "the only appropriate means of giving satisfaction to an officer whose honor was insulted."[13] The officer caste upholds the tradition of dueling as the ultimate means of defending its status.

It is no coincidence that the first mention of dueling occurs in Chapter IV, when Shurochka asks Romashov, "Did you read in the papers about the officers' duel?" (IV, 37), words that quietly point the direction the novel is to take. It is significant too that it is Shurochka — whose preoccupation with status will lead to Romashov's death at her husband's hand — who first brings up the subject. She does not object to the practice of dueling itself — "I realize duels amongst officers are a necessary and reasonable thing," she tells the hero — but to the absurdity of its conditions, which invariably lead to death. Her remarks foreshadow Romashov's own fate: "...some unfortunate lieutenant ... like you, who what's more is the injured party and not the offender, ... is terribly badly wounded in the stomach and dies ... in dreadful agony." But she is convinced that in peacetime duels have a valuable role to play in maintaining army discipline. Her words offer a glimpse of the driving ruthlessness she will later show with fatal effect: "What are officers for? For war. And what's needed most of all in war? Courage, pride, the ability not to turn a hair in the face of death. Where are those qualities most vividly to be seen in peacetime? In duels. And that's all.... And what silly softness it is, this fear of a bullet! It's your job to risk your life" (IV, 38). Immediately after his wife's talk of dueling, Nikolaev asks her for the German for "rival," to which she replies swiftly and correctly *"der Nebenbuhler"*. Kuprin's strategic wordplay affirms that his hero is now unwittingly engaged in a duel with the husband of the woman he loves.

The subject of dueling crops up again in Chapter VIII, during a discussion at the officers' club, where the question is examined in more detail. When Archakovsky admits the unfairness of a system in which the injured party is dismissed from the army if he refuses to fight but is perhaps killed if he does, Bobetinsky interposes pompously that "only blood can wash off the stain left by an insult" (IV, 83). Mikhin and Osadchy express diametrically opposed views of dueling. Tentatively and nervously, in words that echo Romashov's on attacks on civilians in Chapter I, Mikhin argues that each should be treated on its merits. "Sometimes," he stammers, "a duel is useful.... But sometimes ... the highest honor lies in forgiving..." (IV, 85). Osadchy, however, has the last word. Drowning the others out with his powerful voice, he expresses the traditional, sanguinary army attitude: "A duel, gentlemen, must without fail have a serious outcome, otherwise it's an absurdity, ... foolish pity, compromise, leniency, a farce." A duel of the French variety, he adds, where the adversaries exchange shots without hitting each other then shake hands over breakfast, is nonsense and "brings no improvement to our society whatsoever."

The meaning of the novel's title reaches far beyond the collision between Nikolaev and Romashov that concludes it. It embraces not only the hero's inner conflict with himself, good against evil, conviction against officer's duty, but also the wider confrontation between the sensitive individual and the whole of army life. In his unequal struggle against the brutality and philistinism rampant around him, that individual could expect nothing less than annihilation.

V *Romashov*

Like *Moloch, The Duel* sets its hero at center stage, focusing on his feelings and experiences. But unlike Bobrov, whom we find formed *a priori* when that work begins, Romashov develops significantly as the novel progresses. He is the compositional core of the work and from no chapter is he absent. During the two months of the novel's action (early April to early June) we see the rapid sentimental education of a sensitive individual who becomes increasingly aware of the hatefulness of army life. The timid lieutenant of the opening chapter is transformed into a thinking human being acutely aware of the inhumanity of army life and deeply troubled by his own role in it. Kuprin's revelation of his hero's psychology and his damning portrayal of the military are closely dependent on each other. Romashov's moral stature grows in direct proportion to his increasing distaste for the army.

Kuprin's exploration of his hero begins in earnest in Chapter II. However, he makes no attempt to throw light on Romashov's character by offering a detailed biography.[14] Instead, he prefers to reveal facets of his hero's character gradually, through situations and contact with other figures in the novel rather than through direct authorial intrusion.

Romashov's dejection is the inevitable result of provincial army life, its inescapable monotony and squalid boredom symbolized by the clinging mud that squelches underfoot in the remote border town. This first portrait of the hero reveals an inveterate dreamer who takes refuge from reality in romantic fantasies. The chapter begins with his visit to the railway station, the sole source of variety in this wilderness. Suggesting the vistas of possibility that lie beyond Romashov's cramped existence, the railway line appears twice more in the novel as a quietly insistent motif in two crucial meetings (with Nikolaev and Khlebnikov) that confirm his deep involvement in army life. Here the shiny express on its way into Prussia is a fleeting reminder of a very different world, "an inaccessible, elegant, magnificent world where life was an everlasting holiday and celebration" (IV, 19).

Romashov's fantasies owe as much to his childhood, when "all the world was bright and pure" (IV, 56), as to his present adulthood sullied by reality. "In fact," Kuprin notes, "there was still a lot of the child in him" (IV, 21). Gazing at the sunset, Romashov indulges in a familiar daydream tinged with nostalgia for the pristine years of childhood in which it was born: "As always, ... he imagined beyond the bright glow of evening some mysterious, radiant life.... there, far, far beyond the clouds and the horizon flamed ... a miraculous, dazzlingly beautiful city, hidden from view by clouds shot with inner fire. There the roads paved with gold glittered with blinding brilliance, fantastic cupolas and towers with purple roofs rose to the sky, diamonds sparkled in the windows and brilliant, multicolored flags fluttered in the air. And ... in that fabulous, distant city lived joyous, exultant people ... filled with ineffable joy, knowing no bounds in happiness or desire and unclouded by sorrow, shame or care..." (IV, 21).

The fantasy contrasts sharply with Romashov's bitter recollection of the recent episode when Shulgovich shouted at him in front of the ranks. His shame at the insult triggers a reverie full of thoughts of revenge and romantic dreams of martial valor. First he sees himself as a brilliant officer of the General Staff behaving with haughty politeness toward Shulgovich as he bungles the manoeuvres. Next he is called to suppress a workers' riot, and after ordering his men to fire on the mob is decorated for courage. Then he is a spy in Germany, wandering the country and secretly noting details of fortifications and barracks. When captured, he faces a firing squad at dawn with the brave words in fluent German: "Aim at the heart!" (IV, 23). Finally, he imagines himself a colonel in a bloody war with Germany and Austria. On a foaming Arab steed he appears over the hill at the crucial moment to lead the troops to a victory that decides the fate of Russia. Inspired by third rate novels, such daydreams illustrate his naiveté and his illusions about military life. That they persist intact after eighteen months of service even when Romashov himself is fully aware of their emptiness ("What nonsense gets into your head!" [IV, 24]) shows they are simply an escape from reality.

Yet however persistent his dreamings, they do not save him from being degraded by the philistinism of army life. The strict program of self-education Romashov set himself at the start of his military career a year before — the systematic study of French, German, and music — has gone by the board. His cello stands forgotten in a corner, his books gather dust on the shelf, and the papers to which he so eagerly subscribed lie unopened under his desk. He is drinking heavily at the club, is involved in a sordid affair with another officer's wife, has taken to gambling, and grows increasingly tired of the service. Worst of all, he has almost ceased to think. And what thoughts he has are "tedious and confused ... as if there had spread inside his skull a dirty grey spider's web from which he could not possibly disentangle himself" (IV, 25). However, unlike his colleagues, he is aware of his degeneration, and though still too weak to halt it, knows it should stop. In his dreams he visualizes the damage being done him by army life. If his waking fantasies evoke the untainted world of childhood, his sleeping dreams show that his adult self is being destroyed. The process is neatly represented by his vision of a split within him between his younger and older self: the embodiment of purity, the younger Romashov weeps as his older "double" drifts off into the sinister darkness.

Romashov's memories of childhood provide the stimulus for the development of his self-awareness. That development begins in Chapter VI, where Romashov starts to grope toward the consciousness of self that will eventually alienate him from the army. Confined to his quarters on Shulgovich's orders, he is alone for the first time in his eighteen months of service. Suddenly he longs to leave his room for the outside air, "as if he had never known the value of freedom before and now was amazed how much happiness there could be in simply being able to walk where one pleased" (IV, 59). His unfamiliar urge is heightened by the regenerative atmosphere of spring outside his window, with its backdrop of cherry blossom and trees touched with their first greenery. His confinement reminds him of when his mother used to punish him as a child by tying him to his bed by a thread round his ankle. Then, as now, it was not the physical restraint or the fear of punishment that held him captive, but the hypnotic power the thread had over him. To the adult officer Shulgovich's order is now that thread.

His realization that another's will binds him leads Romashov into a protracted inner monologue on the subject of his own self, his "I," his *Ya*. As if understanding this word for the first time, he is staggered by the sudden awareness of his own individuality, the fact of his special identity. Repeating the word over and over again, he becomes aware of the gap between his own self and his environment, between his *Ya* and the *ne Ya:* "I is here inside me ... all the rest is outside and it's not I. This room here, the street, the trees, the sky, the regimental commander, Lieutenant Andrusevich, the service, the flag, the soldiers — all that's not I.... But if I pinch myself on the hand ... that's I. I can see my hand and I lift it up — that's I. What I'm thinking at the moment — that's I too. And if I feel like going out, — that's I" (IV, 61). From his own *Ya* Romashov moves on to recognize the unique individuality of every human being, yet realizes that because each man's *Ya* is closed to his fellow, all of us see others as alien. His thoughts then turn to the men under his command. While each has his own *Ya* and sees in his officer his *ne Ya,* Romashov cannot distinguish his men from one another and sees them only as a mass. His stirrings of social concern are interrupted by the appearance of Gainan, and his thoughts then move in another direction.

This time Romashov's consciousness of his ego leads him to a realization of the futility of army service. In the trivial reasons for his arrest he sees the absurdity of military regulations compared with the ephemerality of his life. In twenty or thirty years, he thinks, his I will be extinguished like a lamp whose wick has been turned down. And what, he asks himself, will he have done with his life, this instant of light in the darkness of eternity? His answer sets in relief the pointlessness of military routine: "I stood to attention, kept my heels together, . . . and shouted. . . : 'Shoulder arms!' " (IV, 62). The superiors who force him to do unnecessary things are mere ghosts who will die with his *Ya.* Nevertheless, they have left their mark on him. "They have insulted and humiliated *Me*", he cries inwardly, "Me! ! ! Why should my I obey ghosts?"

Thoughts of the army lead naturally to thoughts of war. With more naiveté than logic, Romashov concludes that universal resistance to violence would render war impossible. Traditional concepts, he reasons, like duty, honor, and patriotism, have meaning only while he and his I exist. But if those concepts were to vanish, his I would remain inviolable. Therefore his I is more important than all such concepts. And if his I and that of everyone else in the human race were to say "I don't want to!' " war would become unthinkable. So the whole complex edifice of the army, he concludes triumphantly, rests precariously on the fact that "mankind will not, cannot, or dare not say 'I don't want to!' " What then is war, he asks himself, with its death and refined techniques of murder? Is it "a global mistake? Blindness?"(IV, 63).

Gainan's second entry triggers Romashov's earlier thoughts on the individuality of the ordinary soldier. Now his thinking reflects the gulf between him and his men, a gulf it is his duty to bridge: "There are a hundred of them in our company. And each is a man with his own thoughts and feelings, his own particular character and experience of life. . . . Do I know anything about them? No — nothing, apart from their faces. . . . What have I done to bring my soul closer to theirs, my I to their I? — Nothing" (IV, 64). From introspective notions about his own ego, Romashov arrives at an awareness of the plight of the common soldier in his command.

Henceforth the hero's intellectual development goes hand in hand with his increasing concern for his fellow man. Though at this stage the idea of leaving the army does occur to Romashov, he knows he is ill-equipped for civilian life. Unfit for anything else, he is a captive of the army system, a sad fact affirmed by Shurochka's merry call of "Little prisoner!" (IV, 65) beneath his window toward the end of the chapter.

The discrepancy between his lofty thoughts of his ego and his captive situation in the army widens during the scenes that follow. His reprimand from Shulgovich (Chapter VII) demonstrates how insubstantial his self is in practice, as his I must once again submit to another's will. Yet the germ of active retaliation is there. As Shulgovich rebukes him, Romashov feels his whole body tremble; the blood rushes to his face and the room grows dark before his eyes. Filled with hatred, he plunges into a silent blackness, "without thoughts, will, . . . almost without consciousness" (IV, 71), in which there exists only the conviction that any second he will strike his commander across the face. Shulgovich's realization of Romashov's emotional state obliges him to defuse the situation. Conflict in matters military is echoed by social collision. The regimental ball (Chapters VIII and IX) is a ceremonial parade of the vulgarity of army existence. Amid the bogus elegance and affected sophistication of the ball, Romashov is drawn into a tedious verbal duel with his mistress Raisa Peterson, the regimental whore. He now feels ashamed of his affair with this spiteful woman, defiled by his intimacy with her, "as if he hadn't washed or changed his underwear for several months" (IV, 88).

Chapters X and XI show Romashov's increasingly vocal opposition to brutality inflicted on the ranks. His strengthening convictions are expressed in sure, steady words, so unlike his earlier faltering phrases. When Shapovalenko threatens to strike Khlebnikov, Romashov shouts angrily at the corporal: "Don't you dare hit that man! . . . Don't you ever dare do it!" (IV, 103). He restates his opinions even more forcefully in the officers' conversation which follows: "It's disgraceful to hit a soldier . . . who . . . hasn't even the right to lift his hand to ward off the blow" (IV, 105). To Sliva he adds that if he sees him beating soldiers he will report him to the commander. The class in military theory in Chapter XI is a further example of the senseless routine of army life. As its cross-section of soldiers, from the former student Fokin to the bewildered Khleb-

nikov, repeat the formulae required of them, Romashov despairs at
such tedium, and concludes: "it's swinishness to spend one's time
like this" (IV, 111). Now the intricate apparatus of army routine to
which he has given so many years seems "tedious, unnatural, and
contrived, something aimless and idle, born of a general, world-
wide self-deception, something resembling an absurd delirium"
(IV, 112). Again, but now more urgently, he thinks of leaving the
army.

The skillfully maintained tension between Romashov's romantic
notions of himself as a glorious officer and the grim reality of army
life reaches its climax in Chapter XV, when it finally snaps. As the
parade begins, all thoughts of his ego vanish and his feeling is one
of pride at his participation in this stirring spectacle: "suddenly he
felt young, strong, agile, and proud in the knowledge that he too
belonged to this ordered, motionless, mighty mass of men so mysteriously bound together by one invisible will..." (IV, 146). But during the marchpast disaster strikes. Intoxicated by dreams of martial
distinction, he loses his alignment and throws the men marching
behind him into confusion. The chaos of the moment is exemplified
in the pathetic figure of Khlebnikov, struggling along twenty paces
behind and covered with dust. As the brilliant May morning suddenly grows dark before Romashov's eyes, his sense of pride is
reversed: "he felt small, weak, and unsightly, with sluggish movements and unwieldy, clumsy, stumbling legs" (IV, 155). Feeling dis-
graced forever, he resolves to shoot himself.

His shame at his public disgrace turns Romashov's growing
spiritual alienation from his fellow officers into actual physical
isolation. As they return in a group to town, he sets off alone by a
roundabout way, feeling "like some pitiful renegade ... not even a
grown-up man but a loathsome, defective, ugly little boy" (IV,
158). But his shame sharpens his self-awareness by showing him the
similarity between his own experience and that of the common soldier, Khlebnikov. In their own ways, both are victims of an in-
human system. Now Kuprin fuses hitherto separate elements of his
plot: the officer's growing self-awareness and the private's unrelieved suffering. Romashov senses how this day has curiously inter-
twined his own destiny with that of the "wretched, cowed, tormented little soldier" (IV, 159). It is as if they are two cripples, he
thinks, "suffering from ... the same disease and arousing in people ... the same disgust." For all the shame his realization of their
similarity brings, he detects in it "something extraordinary, pro-

found, and truly human." Romashov's identification of himself with the common soldier Khlebnikov is eloquent proof of his alienation from the officer caste.

To cement their spiritual kinship, Kuprin brings Romashov and Khlebnikov physically together in Chapter XVI. The chapter is a triptych embodying the three parallel themes on which the structure of the novel rests. First comes Romashov's meeting with Nikolaev, representing his personal conflict with the officer caste, now intensified by his illicit love for Shurochka. The center of the chapter pivots on Romashov's awareness of self: filled with self-pity, he imagines in melodramatic terms his own suicide and funeral, finding perverse pleasure in the thought of how deeply he would be mourned by his fellows when they saw they had never understood him. The close of the chapter, its third stage, shifts the focus from the hero's self to Khlebnikov. As he looks at the soldier's horribly beaten face, Romashov's own suffering seems trifling beside the other's agony. Yet they have shared the day's disgrace and are equally unhappy. It is now that the motif of human concern reaches its moving crescendo. Filled with compassion, Romashov embraces the sobbing soldier and comforts him. Through the painful chaos of his own emotions — "infinite grief, horror, incomprehension, and profound, guilty pity" — he whispers: "My brother!" (IV, 170). The identification of officer with soldier, man with man, is complete, as both stand bewildered before the senseless savagery of their life.

Yet the rapprochement between them is wholly of Romashov's making, and while he calls Khlebnikov his brother, the soldier continues to address his officer as "sir" (*barin*). Khlebnikov plays a secondary role in the scene, for he says very little and emerges chiefly through the prism of the hero's emotions. Moreover, there is a hint of condescension in Romashov's sympathy, and his words of comfort are "the simple, touching, soothing words an adult uses to a hurt child." Nor is the consolation he offers Khlebnikov — "One must bear it" — anything more than a verbal anodyne. Though dimly grateful, Khlebnikov is almost as bewildered by his officer's compassion as he is by the whole of army life.

However little it does for Khlebnikov, Romashov's conversation with the soldier acts as a catalyst on the confusion of his feelings and brings him maturity overnight. In Volkov's words, the meeting is "a kind of catharsis, a renewal and elucidation of the soul"[15] for the hero, after which everything falls into place. Romashov withdraws from the society of his fellow officers, and now regards people and events around him with sad calm. He has thus been purged of the army in body and soul by his conversation with Khlebnikov, a process suggested by his thoughts of *lustrum*, the ancient Roman purificatory sacrifice. The purgation is followed by his growing association with Khlebnikov, from whom he learns the sorry details of his life both in the regiment and back home. But again it is on Romashov rather than Khlebnikov that we see the effects of their association. The hero's shame at his responsibility as an officer for the soldier's suffering colors his compassion with guilt.

His contact with Khlebnikov proves to Romashov the indubitable individuality yet common suffering of every soldier in his command. With horror he sees that each day brings him face to face with hundreds of "grey" Khlebnikovs, every one of whom has his own joys and sorrows but is depersonalized by "the general servitude of army life, the indifference of his superiors, arbitrariness and coercion" (IV, 172). Worst of all is the realization that not a single officer even suspects that these men are living people, not "mechanical quantities called company, battalion, or regiment."

Like the enforced solitude of his house arrest a month before, Romashov's present voluntary isolation gives him the chance to think. This time he is amazed by the diversity of his inner life, having earlier not even suspected "what joy, what power, what profound interest lay hidden in such a simple, ordinary thing as human thought" (IV, 173). His earlier ideas of leaving the army have crystalized into the decision to resign once he has served the three years required to pay for his education in the Academy. Baffled by the variety of civilian occupations open to him, he concludes that "the vast majority of educated professions are based solely on distrust of human integrity and thus serve human vices and imperfections." Otherwise, he thinks, why should officials like accountants, policemen, and overseers be necessary? As for priests, doctors, and judges, whose professions oblige them to know the sufferings of others, Romashov concludes that such people grow morally callous more rapidly than others. Who then, he wonders, will feed and teach the downtrodden Khlebnikov and say to him: "Give me your hand, brother?" (IV, 174).

Slowly and unsurely, Romashov gropes toward a new view of life. Formerly the world was divided for him into two unequal parts. The smaller consisted of officers who alone possessed the prerogatives of honor, rank, and power. The larger part consisted of civilians, who could be insulted and beaten for amusement. Distanced now from the army by both his disgrace and his convictions, Romashov sees the falsity of such a view, and realizes that "the whole of military service . . . is founded on a brutal, infamous misunderstanding by the whole of mankind." His rhetorical question sums up the novel's evaluation of army life: "How can a class of people exist . . . which in peacetime, without serving the slightest useful purpose, eats other people's bread and meat, wears other people's clothes, lives in other people's houses, and then in wartime goes off senselessly to kill and maim people just like themselves?" (IV, 174).

His reflections lead Romashov to conclude that there are only "three proud callings for man: science, art, and free physical toil." Kuprin suggests that the second will become his hero's *métier*. Romashov's new-found awareness reawakens his interest in his literary work, hitherto only the dabblings of an amateur. Now he dreams of writing a novel to expose all the loathsomeness of army life. But though his thoughts are vivid, they seem pale on paper, and when he compares his efforts to the Russian classics he feels aversion for his own work.

Romashov's self-realization brings with it a decisiveness he has never known before. This and the sudden anger engendered by his pent-up frustration lead to his fight with Nikolaev and the fatal duel. His audacity first manifests itself in a comparatively trivial way, when he flings a bunch of daffodils through Shurochka's bedroom window. But he displays almost reckless courage in the brothel scene of Chapter XVIII. When Bek raises his sword to slash at a whore, Romashov — swept by "a flaming torrent of insane ecstasy and horror" (IV, 185) — seizes Bek's wrist and stops the blow. The outcome of this first duel is entirely positive. Far from hacking Romashov to pieces for his intervention, Bek later squeezes his hand in gratitude.

From Chapter XVIII onward, the personal and environmental factors that have increasingly alienated Romashov from army life coalesce into a fateful force that propels him to his doom. The suicide from Osadchy's company which he is obliged to observe at the autopsy is the harbinger of his own fate, set now as he is on a suicidal collision course with the army. The maelstrom of frenzied drunkenness unleashed by the suicide and inspired by the predatory Osadchy provides the momentum that sweeps the hero to destruction. Drawn into the general orgy by the drunken Vetkin, Romashov finds himself in an intoxicated dream where everything happens "somehow of its own accord" (IV, 179). As his consciousness continually recedes, then fitfully reasserts itself, events follow one another in a sequence devoid of logic, like a nightmare ribbon of film. The episode with Bek is part of this strange delirium, fading into nothing as mysteriously as it flares into being.

Back in the officers' club, the invisible agency controlling the events of this fateful night becomes madness and death itself. Wandering into the guest bedrooms nicknamed "the morgue" because officers have shot themselves there, Romashov stumbles on the alcoholic Klodt and the gambler Zolotukhin drinking themselves insensible in the dark while their drunken colleagues in the next room intone a hymn that resembles a distant dirge. Driven by some incomprehensible force, Romashov returns to his fellow officers, though he knows he should leave. When Osadchy joins the drunken chorus in a maudlin requiem, Romashov, amid sudden silence, shouts angrily at him to stop. The hallucinatory quality of the moment is emphasized by the grotesque shadows cast by the swinging lamp as it turns those present into sinister giants or dwarfs dancing in tangled chaos over walls and ceiling. As all becomes clamorous confusion before Romashov's eyes, the figures tossing around him embody the general delirium, "as if some evil, chaotic, foolish, savagely derisive demon" (IV, 191) has possessed them all. As in a nightmare, things happen with lightning speed and incoherence. Nikolaev's offensive words to Romashov lead to a fight, and the die is cast. Within forty-eight hours Romashov is dead.

Romashov's duel with Nikolaev represents the culmination of his estrangement from his fellow officers. In holding views contrary to theirs, he puts himself beyond the pale of the officer caste. But, as Shulgovich warned him early in the novel, that caste will brook no deviation from its norms: "Watch you don't take us too far. You're only one, while the company of officers is a whole family. That means the one can always ... be grabbed by the tail and thrown out..." (IV, 71). Paradoxically, it is the army that makes of Romashov the thinking individual he becomes. But as he prepares to enter a new life, he is obliged to settle accounts with the old. Whatever his hopes for the future, the army demands retribution in the present, and the gathering gloom of the closing chapters is a reminder that Romashov is doomed. Nemesis stalks *The Duel* from its earliest pages, drawing closer to Romashov with ever more rapid strides. Nikolaev is its embodiment, and his bullet its sentence.

VI *Nazansky*

Nazansky is the most intriguing yet most unsatisfying character in *The Duel.* Though an officer in Romashov's regiment and a close friend of the hero's, he plays no part in events of the novel, and indeed appears in only two chapters (V and XXI), after being first mentioned in Chapter IV during Romashov's visit to the Nikolaevs'. Here Shurochka refers to him several times and reveals that he is a hopeless drunkard who is destroying himself. Her interest in him has more to it than meets the eye, however: afterward Romashov visits Nazansky and discovers that Shurochka and he were formerly in love.

Though we see Romashov and Nazansky together only twice, they belong indivisibly at the philosophical center of *The Duel.* Indeed, it is Nazansky, not Romashov, who enunciates Kuprin's philosophical views in their developed form. In his memoirs Kuprin's friend Batyushkov offers an explanation for the curious closeness of the two characters. The pair represents, he says, the contrasting sides of Kuprin himself. Romashov is the younger of the two, gentle and weak-willed. Nazansky is Kuprin's older self, molded yet battered by life. Influenced by Nietzsche, he has become an individualist who challenges all around him.[16] Batyushkov adds that Kuprin claimed the two men embodied the contrasting character types he inherited from his parents: Romashov stemmed from his mother and Nazansky from the father he barely knew.[17]

The relationship between Romashov and Nazansky recalls that between Bobrov and Goldberg in *Moloch,* with the important difference that while the earlier pair arrive at their conclusions through discussion, here Nazansky does most of the talking and Romashov listens to him largely in silence. On his second appearance, only three chapters from the end of the novel, Nazansky summarizes for Kuprin the detestable features of army life. But he also expresses definite opinions on the very issues with which Romashov only begins to grapple during the novel, and to that extent he is the author's mouthpiece. More educated and talented than the hero, he has also been in the army much longer. He is thus much more damaged by it, serving as "material evidence of the disastrous effect of the officer's life on an intelligent ... man."[18] He acts as confidant for Romashov, who visits him when troubled. But intellectually he is mentor and exemplar too, despite his alcoholism.

Nazansky's importance as a philosophical well-spring in the novel is underlined by the expressive description of him when Romashov first meets him. By an attention to facial detail unparalleled in the work, Kuprin evokes the grace and wisdom of this maverick officer who seems an apostle of light amid the darkness of regimental life. Obliquely too, his statuesque appearance points up Romashov's own facial ordinariness, of which he is so painfully conscious: "Nazansky's ... golden hair fell in large, full curls around his high, open forehead, ... and the whole of his massive, elegant head with the bare neck and open shirt of a noble portrait resembled the head of one of those Greek heroes or sages, whose magnificent busts Romashov had seen on engravings somewhere. His clear, faintly moist, blue eyes had a lively, intelligent, gentle look in them" (IV, 48). Apart from Shurochka, Nazansky is the only physically attractive figure in the novel; through him Kuprin suggests a correlation between prepossessing appearance and intellectual activity.[19]

Philosophically, Nazansky's first conversation with Romashov is much less important than the second, but it prepares the ground for it by outlining his character, touching on his attitude to army life, and revealing the thought and emotion of which he is capable. Nazansky confesses that he hates the army but continues to serve in it because it provides security. Only in drink can he escape the tedium of this "existence as monotonous ... and grey as a soldier's greatcoat" (IV, 46). Only when drunk does he live the miraculous life of his spirit. So full is this life that all he has seen, heard, or read awakes within him and takes on brilliant meaning. Pullulating with myriad encounters and experiences, his memory makes him as rich as Rothschild. In his heightened awareness, he weeps for the joy and sorrow of others. When he first experienced it, this illumination of the spirit seemed like inspiration itself, but now he realizes it is nothing more than the effect of alcohol on his nervous system. But what does it matter, he asks, if drink ruins his health, so long as it brings him such happiness?

Thoughts of women and dreams of love lie at the center of Nazansky's spiritual activity. Often he thinks of the ideal women he can never meet in squalid, provincial army life, those "tender, pure, elegant women ... with snow-white souls who know all and fear nothing" (IV, 48). For him the love of a woman means both boundless delight and acutely sweet suffering. He sees the greatest happiness and torment in unrequited love. His dream when young was to fall in love with an unattainable woman and devote his life to her. What exquisite pleasure, he tells Romashov, to go to any lengths to see his love; what bliss to touch her dress just once in his life. His impassioned words remind Romashov of his impossible love for Shurochka, but also bring Nazansky to confess that he once met such a wonderful woman. Though she ceased to love him because he drank, he loves her still, and lives under the spell of their past intimacy. A letter he shows to Romashov reveals that the woman is Shurochka. Thus both men are involved with her in different ways. But there is no jealousy between them, no duel of rivals. Nazansky is the passive member of the triangle, who now only draws with nostalgia on the emotional reservoir of the past.

Nazansky's second appearance, in Chapter XXI, provides the key to Kuprin's philosophy in *The Duel.* Here his monologue demonstrates his ideological kinship with Romashov, developing the individualist anarchist views Romashov first formulated while under arrest in Chapter VI. If there Romashov groped toward a realization that his own self is the only true reality, from Nazansky he now receives eloquent, if rather confused, confirmation. But while Romashov's thoughts in the early chapter centered on military issues sparked off by his arrest, Nazansky now takes those thoughts to construct a reasonably coherent system applicable to the whole of life. Thus, on the eve of Romashov's duel, Kuprin has Nazansky develop his hero's views as the maturing Romashov would eventually have done had he not been killed. Indirectly, Nazansky's philosophizing, frequently punctuated as it is by Romashov's rapturous words of agreement, underlines the tragedy of the hero's death on the brink of a new life.

From the outset Nazansky urges Romashov to decline the duel, arguing that it would be braver not to fight. Like everything in life, Romashov's pain and hatred will pass, but if he kills his opponent, the dead man's shadow will pursue him forever. By killing his enemy, he will destroy his own *joie de vivre.* Reminding Romashov of the total, incomprehensible *nothing* that awaits man after death, he speaks of the captivating beauty of life, with its music, its scent of flowers, and the sweet love of a woman. But its supreme delight is the "golden sun of life" (IV, 202) — human thought. This is what death destroys, man's "greatest enjoyment and pride . . . that never, never, never will return" (IV, 203).

When Romashov asks what he should do, Nazansky condemns army life in words that not only echo the hero's own earlier sentiments but also distill the essence of the attack on the army mounted by the whole tale: "Just look at our officers.... They're all trash, riff-raff, scum.... Anyone who's talented or able takes to drink. Seventy-five percent ... are infected with syphilis.... To them the service is the object of sheer disgust, a burden, a detestable yoke.... What's vilest of all is the military ambition, the petty, cruel ambition. Men like Osadchy and company who knock out their soldiers' eyes and teeth ... in the service they all become base, cowardly, vicious, stupid, miserable little animals. You ask why? Precisely because none of them believes in the service or sees any sensible point in it" (IV, 203–205).

Nazansky blames this situation partly on the changes wrought in the army by time; in this respect, paradoxically, his views resemble Osadchy's opinions on the degeneration of war. When mankind was in its infancy, war was a joyful intoxication, a valorous, bloody delight. Leaders were chosen for their strength and bravery, and till they were killed their power was regarded as divine. But now mankind has grown older, soldiers are pressed into the army, while the awesome chiefs of old have become functionaries living timorously on wretched pay. Now military valor is tarnished and army discipline gives rise to hatred between officers and men. Nazansky can think of only one other group like the army: the priesthood. It too has degenerated since its beginnings and now the parallels between officer and priest are startling: "There ... the cassock and censer, here the uniform and rattling weapons; there humility, hypocritical sighs, and sickly sweet words, here assumed courage, proud honor, ... and shoulders pulled up high" (IV, 206). Moreover, both groups are parasites on the body social, "like fat lice that grow fatter still on another's body the more it rots." But retribution is close at hand, Nazansky believes, for women will become ashamed of Russian officers and soldiers will cease to obey them. This reckoning will come not only for their brutality over many years, but also for their crass insensitivity, for being "blind and deaf to everything" around them (IV, 207).

Then Nazansky's monologue takes up the individualist anarchist theme earlier adumbrated by the hero. The former seminarist Nazansky rejects the traditional Christian doctrines of humility, obedience, and love of one's fellow men. "Who will prove to me clearly and cogently," he asks, "in what way I am linked with my fellow man — devil take him! — with a mean slave, someone who is diseased, an idiot?" (IV, 208). He loathes the diseased and dislikes his fellow men, so detests most the legend of St. Julian the Hospitaler, in which Julian warms a leper with his naked body in a gesture of supreme selflessness. Self-sacrifice now for mankind of the future means nothing to Nazansky: "What interest will make me smash my own head for the sake of people's happiness in the thirty-second century?"

Love for mankind, he continues, has yielded to a new faith that will survive to the end of time: "This is love for oneself, one's own beautiful body, one's all-powerful mind, the infinite wealth of one's feelings." Nazansky now offers Romashov the kernel of anarchist individualist philosophy: "...just think, Romashov: who is dearer or closer to you than yourself? No one. You are the king of the world, its pride and adornment. You are the God of all that lives. All that you see, hear, and feel belongs only to you. Do what you wish. Take everything you please. Fear no one in the whole universe, because there is no one mightier than you and no one equal to you." When all men possess faith in their own selves, other faiths will become redundant and life will be transformed. Once each individual realizes he is a God, Nazansky believes, human beings will cease to oppress each other, and vice, malice, and envy will disappear from the earth. Purged of the banal, life will become beautiful, "sweet toil, free learning, wondrous music, an easy, gay, perpetual holiday" (IV, 208–209).

While he admits that some might criticize his dreams as "a manifestation of extreme individualism" (IV, 209), Nazansky sees their practical potential: they can bring people together and unite them when the need arises. Since there are some challenges the individual cannot meet alone, he advocates a free association of Godlike individuals to defeat the common enemy. Just such a challenge is posed by what he calls "the two-headed monster" (evidently the imperial eagle): "in it I see everything that binds my spirit, constrains my will, and diminishes my respect for my own person". But the monster can only be defeated through common effort. What is important, he argues, is the force that sets each man beside his fellow: "not sentimental pity for my fellow man but divine love for myself unites my efforts with those of others equal to me in spirit!"

Struggle of this kind is worthwhile, he believes, because it can improve still further a life already immensely pleasurable. Life is a "gay, entertaining, wonderful thing" (IV, 210), he argues at the close of his monologue, and Romashov should not fear it, because hitherto he has seen only one small, dark, unattractive corner of it.

Nazansky urges him to break with the army before it extinguishes the precious light burning within him. That light, his spirit, is the only reality of human existence: "there is only one immutable, beautiful, irreplaceable thing — a free soul, and with it creative thought and a cheerful thirst for life" (IV, 210-11). "Dive boldly into life," he concludes insistently, "and it will not deceive you" (IV, 211).

Nazansky's words crystallize Romashov's earlier thoughts of leaving the army into a resolve to do so ("You're right," he says, "I'll retire to the reserves" [IV, 210]). Whilst he recognizes that much of what Nazansky says is fantasy, he sympathizes with his ideals. Nazansky's monologue takes to their logical conclusion Romashov's earlier thoughts about his self, his fellow men, and life. Not for nothing does he almost say "Farewell, teacher" to Nazansky as he leaves.

In his article on *The Duel,* Gareth Williams points out the striking similarity between Nazansky's views and the main tenets of the individualist anarchist philosopher Max Stirner (pseudonym of Johann Kaspar Schmidt).[20] Williams notes that, though protracted and confused, Nazansky's statements when rearranged express a philosophy much like Stirner's. Indeed, a comparison of Nazansky's words with Stirner's book of 1844, *Der Einzige und sein Eigentum (The Ego and his Own),* reveals close textual parallels.

Nazansky's comments that he has no love for his fellow men and no interest in their welfare except where it coincides with his own parallel Stirner's words: "The egoist's love rises in selfishness, flows in the need of selfishness, and empties into selfishness again."[21] Nazansky's conviction that his own self is the only criterion for action echoes Stirner's "*I* am everything to myself and I do everything *on my account.*"[22] Self-assertion is the driving force behind Nazansky's egoism, as it is for Stirner: "I am *my own* only when I am master of myself, instead of being mastered ... by anything else (God, man, authority, law, State, Church etc.)."[23] At the same time, Romashov's earlier thoughts on the failure of his *Ya* when he was reprimanded by Shulgovich recall Stirner's view: "I deny my ownness when — in the presence of another — I give way, desist, submit."[24] Nazansky and Stirner also coincide on their attitude to property. "Take everything you please," Nazansky urges Romashov, while Stirner says: "I am *entitled* to everything that I have in my power.... If it is right for *me,* it is right."[25] And later he goes on: "To what property am I entitled? To every property to which I — *empower* myself."[26] Both Nazansky and Stirner repudiate the State. While Nazansky advocates a free association of men who are his equals in spirit to defeat the monster of autocracy, Stirner declares he will annihilate the State and "form in its place the *Union of Egoists*."[27] Lastly, both agree that life is enjoyable for the self whose boundless freedom makes him a God-man: Nazansky advises Romashov to dive into life because it is wonderful; Stirner believes "living is . . . in enjoyment."[28]

Thus both Nazansky and Stirner reject all external authority and assert, after Fichte, that "the ego is all."[29] Nazansky is Stirner's egoist, to whom "all things are nothing"[30] and who "lives himself out, careless of how well or ill humanity may fare thereby."[31] Nazansky's (and Romashov's) anarchist views lead Williams to suggest that Kuprin is not concerned with political matters in *The Duel:* "The revolution prophesied by Nazansky is not a political revolution, but a social revolution inspired by the principles of individualist anarchism."[32] Though it is hard to separate social and political elements in Nazansky's program, the uncanny similarity between his propositions and Stirner's suggests the critic's remark is true. And yet a paradox underlies Nazansky's monologue. Whilst professing dislike for his fellow men and indifference to their welfare, he advises the hero to leave the army for his own good before it destroys him. Thus on the eve of his death, Romashov learns from his teacher Nazansky the truth that would have transformed his life: "I am . . . the sole ego: I am unique."[33]

VII *Shurochka*

If anyone puts Nazansky's philosophy of aggressive individualism into practice, it is Shurochka Nikolaeva, whose egoism actually destroys her fellow man. As the woman Romashov loves, she is the linchpin in the confrontation between her husband and the hero, and her ambition sends Romashov to his death.

From the outset Kuprin stresses that Shurochka is very different from other regimental wives. Intelligent and sensitive, perceptive and tactful, she remains aloof from her philistine fellows, their petty scandals and squalid affairs. Our first impression of her is charming. Through Romashov's inner monologue as he watches her knit, her beauty is pictured with a precision rivaled only in the portrait of Nazansky: her pale, passionate face with its burning red lips; her deep blue eyes ringed with yellowish shadow; her small,

light body, so lissom and strong; and the birthmark on her left ear
that resembles the trace left by an earring. But her beauty is only
skin deep. During his first conversation with Romashov, Nazansky
defines the essential trait of her complex soul — consuming ambition: "Perhaps she's never loved anyone apart from herself.
There's a vast lust for power in her, a kind of evil, proud force.
And at the same time she's so good, so feminine, so infinitely nice.
It's just as if there were two people in her: one with a cold, egoistic
mind, and the other with a tender, passionate heart" (IV, 53). Shurochka's intelligence and ruthlessness make her a highly dangerous
animal in the status world of the army. Despising the philistinism of
provincial army life, she is determined her doltish husband shall
enter the Staff Academy so she can escape to the capital. "I need
company," she explains to Romashov, "lights, music, admiration,
subtle flattery, and intelligent people to talk to" (IV, 35). Why,
then, should both Romashov and Nazansky love this ambitious
woman? Perhaps because she possesses the strength of will that
they both lack. With determination and drive, she is making a positive effort to ride out of the quicksand of regimental life on her
compliant husband's back, and secretly both men, especially
Nazansky, admire her for it. Their weakness, indeed, leads Shurochka to reject both of them.

The balance in Shurochka between feminine goodness and evil
pride shifts toward the latter as the novel develops, and pitiless egoism emerges as the dominant, though skillfully masked, trait of her
character. Kuprin shows the process subtly through Romashov's
eyes. Her attitude toward dueling provides the first clue to her
ambition and the callousness that accompanies it. Next comes her
mocking laugh at Romashov during the picnic, when he speaks
shyly of her childlessness, a laugh in which there is "something
instinctively unpleasant that sent a chill breath through Romashov's soul" (IV, 139). In the penultimate chapter, when she comes
secretly to Romashov at night to persuade him to fight the duel, the
baseness of her egoism is revealed in full measure. If earlier she
seemed to him a rare creature from another world, this final meeting shows she is as much a part of regimental life as the cheap
Raisa. Romashov offers to refuse to fight Nikolaev but Shurochka
asks him to go through with the duel, for otherwise her husband's
reputation will suffer and he will never enter the Academy. The
slightest hint of a scandal around Nikolaev's name will shatter her
dream of status. Suddenly Romashov sees all the foulness of her

soul and feels as if "something secret, vile, and slimy had crawled invisibly between them" (IV, 216). The implied image of a snake is reinforced by Shurochka's embracing, coillike arms from which he cannot escape. Her request demonstrates a fundamental difference between them to which Romashov has hitherto been blind. Shurochka herself unconsciously sums it up when she whispers: "You are so pure and good, and I am calculating and vile" (IV, 215). Though she assures Romashov neither he nor Nikolaev will be wounded because she has so arranged things, Kuprin does not reveal whether any understanding actually exists between Shurochka and her husband. Several details toward the close of the chapter, however, suggest there is no such understanding, and that Shurochka is deceiving Romashov. After asking him to kiss her "for the last time," she says tearfully "We'll not see each other again" (IV, 216), then suddenly gives herself to him in a first and last fateful consummation of their love. When she leaves, she bids him not goodbye but "Farewell" (*Proshchai*), and as they kiss Kuprin again emphasizes the chillness of her soul with the words "now her lips were cold and immobile" (IV, 217).

Though he sees the selfish motives behind Shurochka's request, Romashov apparently fights the duel because he believes Nikolaev has come to some agreement with his wife. Since the hero is now aware of Shurochka's baseness, no other reason would seem sufficient to make him face Nikolaev's fire now he has decided to retire from the army. Like his concern for Khlebnikov, his behavior in Shurochka's best interests demonstrates that Romashov cannot follow Nazansky's philosophy to the letter. Yet the final chapter seems to prove that Nazansky is right. By acceding to Shurochka's request, Romashov denies the primacy of his own self, and sacrifices it on the altar of her ego.

VIII *Language and Style*

The importance Kuprin attached to the language and style of his *Duel* is indicated by the many revisions he made in it even after it was submitted for publication. Over one hundred and fifty emendations were carried out and many sentences shortened or cut altogether. Nor did Kuprin stop at the first, *Knowledge,* version of the novel: for the 1912 edition of his works he made over a hundred more changes. After that, however, he left the work as it was.

Kuprin's language in the novel is unprecedentedly rich and flexible. Each character is individualized by his speech or the language of his thoughts, and the work's abundance of dialogue enables us to hear each person's voice. But however much those voices vary, the hall-marks of Kuprin's prose remain invariably simplicity, clarity, and versatility. The latter quality is amply demonstrated by the speech of many officers: the abrupt tone of Shulgovich, who roars at his subordinates; Sliva's stuttering, abusive phrases; the muttering of Lekh with its constant repetition of the word *geto* (evidently for *eto,* "this"); the absurdly affected French of Bobetinsky, supposedly a disillusioned member of the *jeunesse dorée;* and Vetkin's garrulous sentences liberally sprinkled with army jargon and derogatory references to civilians. The soldiers are individualized too. The lesson in theory (Chapter XI) shows Kuprin's skill in identifying characters by their speech peculiarities. He points particularly to the soldiers' tendency to alter words they find hard to pronounce.

Of the gallery of regimental wives in the novel, Shurochka and Raisa are most distinguished by their speech. The powerful precision of Shurochka's language underlines her strength of will and lends her image a firm, masculine quality colored by her emotional outbursts to Romashov. Kuprin's portrayal of the episodic Raisa depends almost wholly on her speech as an indication of character. The grammatical inaccuracy and melodramatic excess of her letters to Romashov reflect the disorder of her morals and the falsity of her soul. The most striking feature of her speech is her affected way of swallowing vowels and her repulsive, adenoidal pronunciation. Thus *"boia bat' grechadka"* is her rendering of *"moia mat' grechanka"* ("my mother is Greek") (IV, 88). Her corrupt speech produced a powerful impression on Tolstoy. "It even gives you heartburn," he said.[34]

Kuleshov points to Kuprin's technique of dividing his sentences into three parts to produce a flowingly rhythmic effect.[35] Most often the division turns on verbs: "The bell rang, the engine whistled, and the gleaming train pulled out of the station" (IV, 19); "He gnashed his teeth, shook his fists, and stamped his feet" (IV, 184). Elsewhere adjectives are thus grouped: "He sensed something novel, festive, and radiant about her" (IV, 124); "he caught its warm, heady, voluptuous smell" (IV, 214). More rarely, adverbs occur in threes: "The soldiers shouted simultaneously, zealously, and loudly" (IV, 146). The triple division of a sentence may be more complex, involving whole phrases: "Romashov slipped through the creaking gate, went up to the wall, and threw the flowers through the window" (IV, 176). Of course Kuprin's sentence structure is not limited to the pattern outlined here. To vary the pace and rhythm of his prose he frequently uses clipped sentences (especially in dialogue) as well as more involved ones that owe nothing to the above technique. Variety is of the essence in his language, as it shifts from the contemplative and sadly lyrical through the tense and emotionally charged to the impassioned and hotly declamatory.

Kuprin sometimes chooses vocabulary for its onomatopoeic value. When Shurochka and Romashov meet in the forest during the picnic, the hero listens to the sounds made by Shurochka as she approaches. The light crackling of branches is followed by the tread of swift steps and the suggestive rustling of petticoats. The description of the band playing at the parade offers sounds of a different kind: "Like mischievous, laughing children, the playful flutes and clarinets ran off in a crowd, the high, brass trumpets cried out in triumphant exultation and broke into song, the muffled beat of the drum hurried their flashing flight, and unable to keep pace with them, the weighty trombones muttered caressingly in their thick, calm, velvety voices" (IV, 146).

Kuprin's style in *The Duel* is varied but unobtrusive. Its dominant element is his continual irony at the melodramatic tendencies of his own early prose. Such tendencies are summed up in Raisa's letter to Romashov in Chapter V, with its talk of his "perfidious deception" and its inaccurate quotation about vengeful Caucasian daggers from Pushkin's poem *The Fountain of Bakhchisaray*. Raisa's style not only characterizes her as a typically overemotional regimental wife, but also parodies the clichés of Kuprin's own early writing. Romashov's habit of thinking of himself in the third person in the bombastic vocabulary of cheap novels serves the same effect: "The eyes of the beautiful, strange lady rested with pleasure on the slim, lean figure of the young officer" (IV, 20). Occasionally Kuprin punctures his hero's romantic dreams with a sharply mocking statement of the truth. As Romashov thinks of himself — "His expressive black eyes glittered with resolution and contempt!" — Kuprin swiftly informs us that "his eyes were not black at all, but the most ordinary-looking of eyes — yellowish with a little green rim round the pupil" (IV, 43).

Verbosity among characters in *The Duel* is rare, and only Osadchy and Nazansky become prolix. The former's tirades are stimulated by drink, but the latter's monologues are his stock in trade whether he is sober or not. With their confused thoughts, frequent pauses and contradictions, Nazansky's monologues convey the complexity of his emotions. Our impression of verbal disorder is intensified by his rapid changes of both pace and style, from the lyrical to the rhetorical and the bombastic to the conversational. Kuprin recognized the bookish flavor of monologues by Nazansky and Osadchy. In 1908 he confessed to a friend: "...some of my favorite thoughts in the mouths of the heroes ... sound like a gramophone (I made this mistake, for example, with Nazansky)."[36] Still, Nazansky's monologues lend *The Duel* its strongly publicistic tone, and it was his calls to freedom that Kuprin quoted so effectively at public readings of the novel in the revolutionary months of 1905.

While Nazansky is revealed primarily through his speech, Romashov is shown chiefly through his inner monologues of varying length and intensity, in which Kuprin elaborates his hero's thoughts and demonstrates his penchant for romantic fantasy. As Berkov notes, in this connection Kuprin resorts to words suggesting the imponderable process of his hero's thought rather than distinct facts, words like "it seemed that...," "as if...," and "he seemed to see...."[37] But apart from his biting remarks to Raisa in Chapter IX and his angry outburst to Nikolaev toward the close, Romashov's speech is as undistinguished as his personal appearance.

In accordance with the neutral quality of most of Kuprin's language, his descriptions are neither extensive nor elaborate, and his restrained prose contains few metaphors or similes. As Kuleshov indicates,[38] many of Kuprin's similes liken his characters to animals, most often to point up the bestiality of the figure concerned. Thus Osadchy, Bek, and Nikolaev are likened to wild animals, and the officers' arrogant contempt for civilians leads Kuprin to compare them to turkey-cocks. Only Romashov's ingenuous orderly Gainan is granted a sympathetic animal simile, when Kuprin compares him to a clumsy young puppy. Other similes are striking for their unusualness: the clinging mud in the town is compared to Turkish delight, and cherry trees in blossom resemble a throng of little girls in white dresses. A very effective image is found in Chapter XVIII, where the lonely Romashov feels irresistibly attracted to the brothel, "as on a cold night weary, frozen birds of passage are drawn to the beacon of a lighthouse" (IV, 180).

Kuprin's treatment of nature deserves brief mention. Like the material portrayal of military and domestic settings, he uses nature description sparingly. It appears almost exclusively in connection with the three main characters (Romashov, Nazansky, and Shurochka), and is most often seen through the eyes of the hero, for whom nature serves as a "litmus paper"[39] that clarifies his emotions both for himself and the reader. Thus the spring morning makes Romashov's house arrest seem more onerous still, while the innocent beauty of the dawn after his fight with Nikolaev makes him feel base and vile. But it is in the forest scene in Chapter XIV that Kuprin is at his descriptive best. As Romashov and Shurochka lie in the grass talking of love, the blood-red sunset flaring ominously in the sky symbolically foreshadows the fatal clash between the hero and Shurochka's jealous husband.

Several of Kuprin's literary contemporaries praised his writing in *The Duel*. "His language is beautiful and very graphic," said Tolstoy, "he doesn't overlook anything that might ... produce an impression on his reader."[40] Gorky was no less vocal in his commendation, and pointed to the immense improvement in Kuprin's language. In a letter of 1911 to a young writer, Gorky advised him to learn linguistic skill from great authors like Turgenev and Chekhov, adding that Kuprin had followed this advice with great success — "Take his language before *The Duel* and after, and you'll see what I mean...."[41]

IX *Critical Response*

The publication of *The Duel* produced a furore among both critics and the reading public, and the ensuing controversy continued till 1917. Most commentators saw the novel as an attack not only on the army but on autocracy itself. The military evils revealed by Kuprin were symptoms of the incurable disease afflicting the whole of Russia. Thus the work attracted critical attention more for the social and political issues it raised than for its literary qualities.

Journalists and critics were sharply divided in their responses: those of liberal and radical persuasion welcomed *The Duel* as another nail in the coffin of autocracy, while their conservative and reactionary fellows condemned it as a perfidious assault on the ruling order. One progressive critic wrote of the "fatal rust" eating away at the apparatus of militarism and preparing its inevitable ruin.[42] Gorky wrote that Kuprin had done all thinking officers a service by showing how isolated they were as a caste: "He has helped them ... recognize ... their position in life, to see all its abnormality and tragedy."[43] Many reactionary critics saw in *The Duel* an outright slander on the Russian army. One described the work as "a most indecent lampoon full of slovenly insinuations, ... calculated to make some soldiers ashamed of their profession."[44] Needless to say, the vast majority of officers were incensed by the novel, and one even challenged Kuprin to a duel through a Petersburg paper.[45] On the other hand, in the summer of 1905 a group of twenty officers wrote to Kuprin expressing their gratitude for the novel, and commenting that the sores on the body military required fundamental treatment of a kind only possible if the whole of Russian life were transformed.[46] But such views were highly exceptional among the military. One general condemned *The Duel* as a malicious attack on the army inspired by the treacherous Gorky.[47] In 1910 there appeared an entire pamphlet on the novel, recognizing the truth of much of what Kuprin had written, but still accusing him of distortion in his picture of the army.[48]

In their attempts to denigrate the novel, several critics maintained that it portrayed some specific regiment, and that its picture of the army was not representative. In an article of 1906 for a Vienna paper, Kuprin denied having had a particular regiment in mind.[49] The episodes in his novel derived, he said, from varied situations in the army, and no character was drawn from his own regiment.[50] He concluded the article by predicting a bloody holocaust in which all Russia would rise in rebellion. Little did he know that in just over a decade his prophetic words were to prove correct.

X   *Unrealized Further Plans*

Kuprin was dissatisfied with the ending of *The Duel,* and for years could not consign Romashov to the past. He felt the closing chapters were badly written because he had been so rushed. He had wanted to describe the duel between Nikolaev and Romashov, but pressure of time had forced him to end the work with the brief duel report instead.[51] Two years after the novel's publication, he offered a Moscow publisher an "unwritten chapter" of *The Duel.* It would show, he said, Romashov's thoughts and feelings at the duel, and that "at the last moment ... he realizes unerringly Nikolaev ... will kill him."[52] Such a chapter would have severely weakened the dramatic effect of the novel's finale, and it is fortunate that the publisher refused it.

A more serious problem, however, was that in killing his hero, Kuprin had robbed himself of the possibility of writing a sequel to *The Duel* with Romashov as its central character, a possibility suggested by Romashov's decision to resign his commission. Kuprin went so far as to plan a sequel — the novel *Nishchie (The Beggars)* — but realized that without alterations to the end of *The Duel* the project was impossible: "Romashov, recovered from serious wound, retires to the reserves ... and ... leaves for what seems to him a bright, new future. And now here he is in Kiev. . . . But Romashov — my double — is killed, and I can't write *The Beggars* without him."[53] Seeing the autobiographical nature of the projected novel, Gorky strongly disapproved of Kuprin's plans to resurrect Romashov and urged him to direct his energies to something new.[54] *The Beggars* never became much more than an idea, so *The Duel* remained as it was, entire and whole, marking the summit of Kuprin's career and assuring him immortality in the annals of Russian literature.

CHAPTER 5

1905 and After

I Echoes of 1905

THROUGHOUT his life Kuprin was a man of indefinite political views that he rarely expressed in his writing. But the events of 1905 moved him to declare himself, and in several works of this time he adopted a progressive position openly critical of the regime.

His first response to this year of foreign war and domestic repression was his sketch "Pamiati Chekhova" ("To the Memory of Chekhov"), commemorating the first anniversary of Chekhov's death. Published only two months after *The Duel*, the work is pervaded by the revolutionary enthusiasm of those days, when the collapse of tsarism seemed imminent. Beside the bloody horror of the Russo-Japanese War, Chekhov's charm seems like a distant fairy tale. But now, as freedom draws near, Kuprin recalls the "fragrant, delicate, sunlit" words (IX, 97) with which Chekhov spoke of the brighter future for mankind. All things come to an end, he writes, and everyone believes that Russia will emerge renewed from the bloodbath of 1905, that her people will breathe the air of freedom and see the diamond-studded sky of which Chekhov dreamed. Imprecise though Kuprin's ideas are — he does not specify *how* the new life will come about — they indicate his profound concern for Russia at this crisis point in her history.

December of 1905 saw Kuprin's most virulent denunciation of repression in his angrily publicistic sketch "Sobytiia v Sevastopole" ("Events in Sevastopol"), in which he describes the destruction of the cruiser *Ochakov* in Sevastopol harbor that November. The mutiny on the *Ochakov* lasted five days, ending on November 15 when the cruiser was shelled, with the loss of hundreds of lives. Kuprin was in Balaklava at the time and actually witnessed the event. Appalled at the spectacle of senseless slaughter, "that bonfire of human flesh" (III, 438), he directs his attack at

Admiral G. P. Chukhnin, commander of the Black Sea fleet, who ordered the ship shelled and forbade the rescue of survivors. "Until I die," writes Kuprin in pain and fury, "I shall never forget that . . . vast blazing vessel, that last word in engineering, condemned to death together with hundreds of human lives by the extravagant will of one man" (III, 440). In urgent prose he describes the confused flight of people from Sevastopol, the horrified crowds hopelessly watching the cruiser burn, and the piercing shrieks of men being burnt to death.

Chukhnin reacted quickly by ordering Kuprin to leave Sevastopol within forty-eight hours and then instituting legal proceedings for slander. Though Chukhnin was assassinated in June 1906, the case was still heard two years later. Sentenced to a fine or ten days' house arrest, Kuprin chose the latter and served his sentence in Zhitomir in August 1909. His role in the *Ochakov* affair, however, was not confined to that of angry journalist. His later tale "Gusenitsa" ("The Caterpillar," 1918) reveals that he helped to rescue several sailors who escaped from the blazing cruiser.[1]

From one instance of heinous repression, Kuprin moved on to show the agony of all Russia in the iron grip of reaction. Published on December 25, 1905, his miniature "Sny" ("Dreams") is an impassioned monologue on the suffering of his native land. He looks upon his "wretched, beautiful, amazing, incomprehensible homeland" and sees in her "a beloved woman, dishonored, mutilated, bloodstained, outraged, and betrayed" (III, 445). The immeasurable vastness of Russia is ablaze with fires, running with blood, and littered with corpses, while the earth shudders with groans as bestial gangs laughingly slaughter old men, women, and children. Kuprin believes that soon this nightmare will end, though again, as in the piece on Chekhov, he fails to show how the transformation will occur. One day, he believes, amid the violence and bloodshed, "someone's calm, wise, grave word will resound — a comprehensible, joyous word" (III, 445–46), and men's eyes will be opened. Then hunger and suffering will vanish and men will be equal and free. The dawn of freedom draws near, he concludes: eternal glory to those who wake us from our bloody dreams, and eternal memory to those who have died.

While "Dreams" illustrates the suffering of Russia in 1905, the tale "Tost" ("The Toast"), of January 1906, demonstrates Kuprin's belief in the eventual triumph of universal freedom. Set on New Year's Eve in the year 2905, it shows an ideal world where all men are united in "a universal, anarchical union of free people" (IV, 219) reminiscent of that proposed by Nazansky. Miracles of technology have transformed the earth, quadrupling the productivity of her soil and turning the whole planet into a blossoming garden. Tyranny, violence, and deception are now unknown, work is a delight, love beautiful and free, and death no longer feared. Recalling the revolution in the twentieth century long ago, Kuprin's engineer-orator is horrified at the monstrous life of their forefathers, who knew only disease, vice, and filth. Yet that ugly age gave birth to revolutionaries who sacrificed their lives for the future of mankind. That river of blood swept mankind out into the sea of universal happiness. But in the closing lines the motif of gratitude to past revolutionaries that sounded at the end of "Dreams" is given a thought-provoking twist. As the orator proposes a toast to freedom's martyrs, a woman of rare beauty beside him weeps with yearning for those distant days of heroism. Struggle and self-sacrifice, Kuprin implies, are mankind's suprime joys, and beside them the rarest felicity seems wanting.

That joy lies in revolutionary struggle is the message of Kuprin's parable "Iskusstvo" ("Art," 1906), in which he examines the link between art and revolution. Asked how one can combine art and revolution, a sculptor flings back a curtain to reveal the figure of a slave straining to burst his chains. While one spectator finds the work beautiful, and a second lifelike, the third exclaims: "Oh, now I understand the joy of struggle!" (IV, 307). Kuprin was convinced that art should not only be beautiful and realistic, but should inspire positive thoughts of freedom.

As pieces like "Dreams" and "Events in Sevastopol" show, violence is the most insistent motif in Kuprin's work immediately after 1905. His tale "Ubiitsa" ("The Murderer," 1906) is interesting since it offers a psychological explanation for the bloodshed that swept Russia in 1905. Amid a general conversation on contemporary violence — "executions and shootings, people burnt alive, women dishonored, old men and children murdered" (IV, 262) — the narrator of this story within a story tells of a murder on his conscience. Ten years ago he was obliged to shoot a cat that had lost a leg in a trap. But shot after shot failed to kill it, and in the end a peasant stopped the butchery by simply swinging the cat against a beam. What horrifies the narrator to this day is not the shooting itself — after all, he has hunted animals and fought in war — but the "chill, terrible, insatiable urge to kill" (IV, 265) that drove him to fire again and again. From the depths of his soul, he recalls, "some dark, vile, . . . terrible force" (IV, 266) suddenly rose and swamped his reason. This same bloody fog, he argues, takes possession of those who visit violence upon Russia today. Though sick with blood, they cannot help themselves, for they are possessed of a "devil with lacklustre eyes and clinging flesh." And as they kill, they feel neither pity nor repentance, for their brains are wrapped in bloody delirium. There is only one consolation, he concludes. Down the years these wretched men will never forget the horrors they have committed, and even in their death-agony will remember the blood they have shed.

II   *"Staff-Captain Rybnikov"*

Whereas works like "Events in Sevastopol" focus on the domestic Russian scene, the tale "Shtabs-Kapitan Rybnikov" ("Staff-Captain Rybnikov," 1906), though set in Petersburg, has a close bearing on the Russo-Japanese War on the Pacific. Its opening sentence sets it precisely on the infamous day of Tsushima (May 27, 1905), when the Russian fleet was destroyed by the Japanese. The work tells of a Japanese spy who poses as the Russian soldier Rybnikov and gathers information by visiting government departments ostensibly to secure financial assistance as a wounded veteran. Kuprin had long been intrigued by the notion of a spy carrying out his lone mission in the heart of an enemy nation. In his dreams of valor Romashov had seen himself as a spy in Germany. Kuprin's Rybnikov was based on an officer of that name whom he met in one of his favorite haunts, the "Capernaum" restaurant in Petersburg. The real Rybnikov was a Siberian, wounded at the battle of Mukden, whose Mongolian features reminded Kuprin of a Japanese.

Through Rybnikov's talk of the war Kuprin reveals the incompetence of the Russian army in the field. Those in command fail to adapt to the terrain, their men are supplied with shells of the wrong caliber and obliged to fight for days without food, while their officers play cards and take mistresses. All the while the Japanese fight with the efficiency of machines. Morale is disastrously low in the Russian ranks, and mutiny increasingly apparent. More ferment still is to be seen in the navy, where officers are afraid to meet their sailors ashore. Through the military bureaucrats whom Rybnikov visits, Kuprin points ironically to the reasons for Russia's defeat in the Far East. "And that's what Russian officers are like!" they exclaim. "Just look at that fellow [Rybnikov]. Well, surely it's clear why we're losing one battle after another? Dullness, stupidity, complete absence of any self-respect. . . . Poor Russia!" (IV, 225).

But "Rybnikov" draws its power not from the hero's espionage activities (of which we see little), but from the tense psychological duel between him and Shchavinsky, a journalist convinced that Rybnikov is a Japanese spy yet unable to prove it. Shchavinsky is clearly a self-portrait by Kuprin. A "collector of human documents, . . . of rare and strange manifestations of the human spirit" (IV, 234), he strives to penetrate the innermost recesses of another's soul, "to hold in his hands a warm, live human heart and feel it beating" (IV, 235). What fascinates him about Rybnikov is the incredible presence of mind of this man who in broad daylight in an enemy capital plays the garrulous Russian soldier with unrelenting skill. At any moment the slightest mistake can destroy him. To the journalist Rybnikov exhibits the very highest degree of patriotic heroism. But all his efforts to make Rybnikov reveal his true identity fail. And yet, like a good detective writer, Kuprin leaves clues that prove Shchavinsky right: Rybnikov's fine silk linen of a kind Russian soldiers never wear, his excessively deliberate pronunciation, the superfluity of Russian proverbs in his speech (some of them not quite apropos), and the warm gleam in his eye at the word *samurai.*

Though artistically both necessary and satisfying as the culmination of the psychological struggle between Shchavinsky and Rybnikov, Kuprin's denouement is unfortunately melodramatic. Moreover, the story's pace is slowed by the unnecessarily detailed treatment of the thief Lenka in Chapter VI, which serves no useful purpose in the finale two pages later. In a stylish brothel, Rybnikov gives himself away by shouting *Banzai!* in the arms of a whore, leaps from her window, breaks his leg, and is caught. But despite its melodrama, the closing scene is intensely powerful. Discovered now, Rybnikov instantly reverts to his real Japanese self. Pale but totally calm, his wounded soldier's limp gone, with soft, catlike movements he prepares to escape, whispering to the whore that he will kill her if she moves. When seconds later, he lies in defeat in the yard below, his eyes burn with implacable hatred.

III   *"The River of Life"*

If "Rybnikov" points to military incompetence, "The River of

Life" (1906) is an indictment of the social conditions in Russia that cripple the capacity of the young for effective revolutionary action. The tale falls into two sections. The first and longer section describes the setting of the work and the characters who belong to it. But it is the second section, the closing chapter (IV), that constitutes the kernel of the tale.

In the squalid Kiev hotel "Serbia" the grasping proprietress Anna Fridrikhovna lives a life of philistine vulgarity and moral laxity. Her shabby establishment is frequented by undistinguished visitors to the city: petty brokers, priests, and pilgrims, or couples who rent a room for an hour or a night. Its only permanent residents are prostitutes. With the proprietress live her lover Chizhevich, a seedy reserve lieutenant, and her four children, precocious as a result of the vice around them. This is especially true of thirteen year old Alechka, whose nascent sexuality is expressed in her adult eyes and strangely voluptuous smile. Banality reigns in stifling triumph in the "Serbia," pervading the lives of its inmates like the smell of kerosene and boiled cabbage that drifts through its proprietress's room.

Framed by the stagnation of this vacuous existence is the suicide of an anonymous student, who takes a room, asks for paper and ink, then shoots himself. At least, such is the sequence of events as the proprietress sees them. But inside the student's room, Kuprin looks over his shoulder as he writes his suicide letter, and through it reveals its writer's character. Having betrayed his revolutionary comrades in a cowardly manner under interrogation, the student has resolved to kill himself, and writes an explanation. The reason for his cowardice, he writes, lies in the circumstances of his upbringing during the reactionary 1880s. His mother is to blame for his subservience to all those in authority. Widowed early, she was forced to depend on charity, and so the student's earliest memories are of her obsequiousness before her benefactors. (Compare Kuprin's suffering at his own fatherless childhood and his mother's straitened circumstances.) As a boy he hated and feared those condescending benefactors, just as he now hates and fears "all complacent, stereotyped, sober people who know everything in advance" (IV, 281), people like professors, archpriests, and radical women doctors whose hearts are as cold as a marble slab. His years in a charitable boarding school only reinforced his servility, so that when his mind became receptive to dreams of freedom, his soul was already devastated forever by "base, neurasthenic timidity"

(IV, 282). Like his whole generation, he despises slavery, yet is a slave himself. His hatred of servitude is passionate but fruitless, like the love of a eunuch.

This, then, is why he will shoot himself, not so much for betraying his comrades as for being a slave to cowardice in these terrible days when it is shameful to be so. Reflecting on his imminent death, he feels that nothing is irrevocably lost in this world, and that all our deeds, words, and thoughts live on in others after we have gone. These are streams that flow together to form the invincible river of life. The time will come, he believes, when that river will wash away all constraints on the freedom of the spirit, and where once "there was a sandbank of vulgarity (*poshlost'*), will be the greatest depths of heroism" (IV, 284). In a moment his life too will join that river, and perhaps within a year will help to drown this vast city and obliterate its name forever.

Kuprin surrounds his hero's closing lines with mounting tension as the clock ticks away and a dog barks rhythmically in the yard below. On the stroke of nine, as he promised himself, the hero pulls the trigger. But the tragedy of his suicide and all it signifies reaches no further than the room in which it occurs. With delicate symmetry Kuprin closes his tale as he began it: while the student's body lies in the anatomy theatre, Anna Fridrikhovna tipsily dances an after dinner polka with Chizhevich and the local policeman. Vulgarity and indifference are in the "Serbia" to stay.

IV   *Anecdote, Fable, and Legend*

From the tragic suicide of an unwritten casualty of revolution, Kuprin turned to a situation full of wry humor amid the frightening chaos of 1905. "An Insult" (1906) is, in Vorovsky's words, "a tale imbued with the ... growing feeling of human dignity characteristic of that time."[2] Set in Odessa and subtitled "a true occurrence," it describes the visit of a delegation of professional thieves to a commission of lawyers dealing with the victims of the latest Jewish pogrom. The thieves are insulted by newspaper accusations that they have participated in pogroms at the bidding of the police, and ask the lawyers to refute this calumny, which soils their reputation as "honest" thieves.

The tale is a subtle fusion of outright comedy and lacerating social criticism. The amusing speech made by the spruce gentleman-thief explains the rationale behind his profession and reveals its attractions. Repeating Proudhon's maxim that "property is robbery," the orator argues that theft acts as a corrective mechanism in a society where wealth is concentrated in few hands. At the same time, the profession of thief combines all the traditional elements of art — "vocation, inspiration, imagination, inventiveness, ambition, and a long, hard apprenticeship" (IV, 292). But under cover of this sparkling oration and the amusing demonstrations of thieves' skill that accompany it, Kuprin attacks both the police and the regime for their role in the pogroms. Hiring a rabble of drunkards and hooligans, the police openly incite them to slaughter innocent Jews. But the police and the mob are not primarily responsible for this evil. Behind them, autocracy itself whips them to hysteria and makes of them "a senseless fist ... incited by a devilish will" (IV, 302). By a neat paradox Kuprin lays bare through that traditional pariah, the thief, the hypocrisy of "respectable" Russian society in the early 1900s.

Fables and legends were a genre to which Kuprin resorted throughout his career because of their allegorical potential. Such in 1906 were the fairy tale "Schast'e" ("Happiness"), which asserts the immortality of thought, and "Legenda" ("The Legend"), a romantic tale of vengeance and death. More important in the context of 1905 is the eastern legend "Demir-Kaya" (1906), which develops the theme of betrayal central to "The River of Life." The robber Demir-Kaya has ninety-nine murders on his conscience, but is forgiven them all by Allah for killing a single traitor, who was about to betray the conspiracy of his friends to overthrow their cruel pasha. Readers at the time could hardly miss the parallel between pasha and tsar, still less Kuprin's implication that the overthrow of a tyrant is a righteous cause.

"Bred" ("Delirium,"1907) uses the biblical legend of Cain to cast new light on the horrors of reaction. The tale is a reworked version of "Ubiitsy" ("The Murderers") of 1901, set in South Africa during the Boer War. While preserving his original New Year's Eve setting, Kuprin changes the name of his principal character to Captain Markov, and transfers the action to Russia in the months after 1905, when punitive expeditions brought bloodshed to many rural areas. This topical story is a compressed psychological study of the emergence of shame and repentance in Markov at his punitive activities. In its half-dozen pages he changes from a brutal officer who proudly defends the might of Russia to a thinking human being racked by guilt. The reason for his transformation lies in a strange old man Markov orders to be shot at dawn as a spy. When told of his fate, the mysterious prisoner only smiles at the captain in indifference and pity. During the night the old man appears to Markov as the soldier tosses in delirium and reveals that he is the eternal witness of all bloody killings since the dawn of history. He was beside Napoleon at Austerlitz and Borodino, with the Catholics as they slaughtered the Huguenots on St. Bartholomew's Night, walked in the wake of Attila and Genghis Khan, and heard the lamentation of the Jews at the fall of Jerusalem. He is, in fact, Cain himself, the world's first murderer, cursed by God and condemned to wander the earth forever. Forced to witness all human slaughter, the first fratricide now sees in every killing Abel's corpse stretched out on the sand. Horrified by his sudden awareness of his participation in universal carnage, Markov resigns his command. In abstract but effective terms, Kuprin's tale condemns not only the gratuitous bloodshed of the reactionary years, but all violence perpetrated by man upon his fellow.

V   *"Gambrinus"*

Kuprin's tale "Gambrinus" (1907) is an emotional summation of many motifs of his writing after 1905. Echoing the declamatory tone of "Events in Sevastopol," it presents a paradigm of events in Russia from the turn of the century to after the first revolution. Days of peace are followed by the unpopular war with Japan; the euphoria of 1905 yields to the riots and pogroms of the years of reaction. Against this historical background, Kuprin traces the growth of dignity in his little hero Sashka, whose musical gift asserts the joy of struggle illustrated by the parable "Art."

As usual, on a base of solid reality Kuprin erects a structure in which fact and fiction are inextricably interwoven. The locational fulcrum of the work is the Odessa tavern, "Gambrinus," of which Kuprin had fond memories. Sashka, the Jewish musician who embodies the spirit of the tavern, was a genuine figure familiar to all Odessa.[3] The city is an all-embracing presence within the tale. After describing briefly the center of Odessa, with its festive shop windows and majestic policemen, Kuprin turns his eye on the colorful port to produce a masterpiece of evocative description. Though poor and squalid, the harbor is a fascinating world of steep, narrow streets crowded with countless taverns, gambling dens, and brothels. Cosmopolitanism is the hallmark of this bustling venue for ships of every nation on the globe. The varied denizens of this quarter are no less intriguing, and Kuprin speaks of them with profound affection. Fishermen, sailors, engineers, stevedores, smugglers — all are "young, healthy, and steeped in the strong smell of the sea and fish" (IV, 342). He openly admires the vigorous intensity of their simple lives, the burden of toil they all bear, and the frenzy of their revelry ashore. The "Gambrinus" is the center of their harsh existence, for it offers oblivion after their labors. In its dank, crowded room they sing and dance to the music of Sashka's violin with the easy spontaneity of natural folk. In the Gorkian manner, Kuprin sees in his simple people an elemental spiritual purity that derives from the uncomplicated nature of their life of toil.

Music lends power to "Gambrinus" as it constitutes Sashka's raison d'être. Referring to historical events only in general terms, Kuprin uses his hero's music to trace the changes of mood among his audience during the early 1900s. Sashka is a folk artist whose vast repertoire is able instantly to suit his audience's need for music gay or sad, a need that depends directly on events of the moment. During the Boer War he plays the "Boers' March," a hymn to their struggle for liberation from the British yoke; at the time of the Franco-Russian friendship celebrations, he plays the "Marseillaise." But the outbreak of war with Japan brings a sudden change of tempo. When at first victory seems certain, the cheerful "Kuropatkin March" resounds from Sashka's fiddle, but then successive Russian defeats are reflected in the refrain of the fishermen's mournful song about recruitment for the Far East. After Sashka has returned miraculously from captivity in Nagasaki, the 1905 revolution arrives with its "radiant, festive, jubilant days" (IV, 357), and Sashka plays the "Marseillaise" again. Now the emotive swell of "Gambrinus" rises to a crescendo and the tale ripples into its swift coda. During the months of reaction after 1905, Sashka refuses to play the national anthem when ordered to do so by a thug, and his left arm is brutally crippled by the police so that he can never play the violin again. Yet music triumphs over all in the finale: undaunted by his mutilation, Sashka thrills his audience once again, this time with a flute.

Sashka's role in the tale develops the idea of "Art" (written simultaneously with "Gambrinus") that true creativity serves a social purpose. That creativity is revealed in the closing lines, as Sashka's audience whirls in a gay dance to the sound of his flute, a scene Kuleshov describes as "the apotheosis of the power and might of the humble musician, the triumph of his talent."[4]

Sashka's music expresses the emotions of his time, and though Kuprin leaves his twice-resurrected hero in the dark days of reaction, Sashka's music and its power to move men's hearts remain invincible. "A man can be crippled," the last line asserts, "but art endures and conquers all" (IV, 362).

VI   Political and Social Satires

Not all Kuprin's works of the immediate post-1905 period are permeated with the tragedy of those years. Several pieces of this time contain a satirical treatment of contemporary political events. Such are the two topical "Skazochki" ("Little tales"), entitled "O dume" ("On the Duma") and "O konstitutsii" ("On the Constitution"), published in March 1907. Bearing the descriptive subtitle "adapted by children for their parents," the tales are playfully allegorical thrusts at the first and second state Dumas (parliaments) of 1906 and 1907 and at the constitution promised by the tsar's October Manifesto of 1905.

"On the Duma" shows Kuprin's hostility to an assembly whose membership was heavily weighted in favor of the wealthier classes. His Duma deputies are well-dressed "children of the nobility" who, after much persuasion, allow an urchin to join their game. Once admitted to the company of his social superiors, the urchin plays tricks on them, dirtying their fine clothes and abusing them before running off in triumph. When his victims' noble parents threaten him, the urchin defiantly sticks out his tongue at them. All this, warns Kuprin in conclusion, is only the beginning; the real story is yet to come.

"On the Constitution" is closer to the fable and recalls the work of the nineteenth century fabulist Ivan Krylov. To Kuprin, the constitution proclaimed in the 1905 manifesto is a deception, like a piece of beef tied to a long string and fed by a boy to a chained, starving dog. Each time the dog swallows the meat the boy pulls it back again. Eventually the infuriated animal breaks its chain, bites the boy, and eats the meat. Now that it has tasted freedom, the dog can never be chained again.

From compact political allegory, Kuprin turned to more elaborate social satire. The tales "Mekhanicheskoe pravosudie" ("Mechanical Justice") and "Ispoliny" ("The Giants"), both of 1907, attack the rabid reactionary who resists all social change and longs for the good old days when "the rod and morality walked hand in hand" (IV, 394). As in "A Quiet Life," Kuprin's satire in both works is aimed at a complacent pedagogue who is the epitome of conservatism. In "Mechanical Justice," however, the subtle irony of "A Quiet Life" yields to outright farce: as the teacher demonstrates to his audience the mechanical flogging machine he has invented, his brainchild traps him and thrashes him within an inch of his life. Transformed by his experience, the sadistic zealot becomes a gentle melancholic loved by his pupils. Through his hero's grotesque invention, Kuprin points not only to the cruel use of corporal punishment in Russian schools but to the vast, brutal apparatus of Russian autocracy itself.

"The Giants" is more condensed and its satire more biting. Its hero, the captious pedagogue Kostyka, preaches blind obedience to authority and denounces all current interests of the young, be they Marx, Nietzsche, freedom, or the proletariat. Returning home embittered and drunk after a party, he subjects the portraits of the Russian writers on his walls to an examination as he would his schoolboys. Through the criteria Kostyka applies to these literary giants, Kuprin scathingly reveals his obscurantist hero's attitudes. Disapproving of Pushkin's ode "Freedom," Kostyka awards him a "nought with double minus" for his poetry and a "one" for his "un-Christian feelings" (IV, 396). To Lermontov he gives a "three minus" for talent; noughts for conduct, attention, and scripture, and a "one" for his morals. Gogol fares better. Though he gets a nought for ridiculing the powers that be, he is awarded a "four" for abusing the Jews and a "five" for his repentance before death. Next, Kostyka reproaches Turgenev for his love for a foreign woman and Dostoevsky for his sectarianism. But then Mikhail Saltykov-Shchedrin pronounces Kuprin's verdict on his reactionary pedagogue: when Kostyka reaches the satirist's portrait,the great man utters in a voice hoarse with anger: "Slave, traitor and..." (IV, 397). The foul but deleted word which follows, Kuprin tells us, is only used to express extreme repugnance. In the best traditions of satire, Kuprin turns the knife by bringing his satirical figure to see himself as he really is.

VII *"Emerald"*

Kuprin's overtly political works inspired by 1905 were followed by others with no bearing on events of that time. Many treat universal motifs such as human love and the joy of being alive in a wondrously beautiful world. This difference of emphasis indicates that — despite the assertions of some Soviet critics to the contrary — Kuprin was never an *engagé* revolutionary bard like Gorky. The fact is underlined by his reaction to Gorky's insistence that he turn to immediate social issues after completing *The Duel:* "He was hoping to make me into a herald of the revolution.... But I was not filled with the fighting mood."[5] Kuprin's departure from *Knowledge* and his estrangement from Gorky after 1908 are further proof of the political vacillation that characterized his career. His deteriorating relationship with Gorky was not helped by the publication in 1908 of Kuprin's tale "Morskaia bolezn' " ("Seasickness"), which tells of the rape of its Social Democrat heroine, a work Gorky regarded as a deliberate slur on the SD Party.[6]

Kuprin's first significant nonpolitical work after 1905 was his tale "Izumrud" ("Emerald," 1907), the most famous of his animal stories. Always fond of animals, he believed that man could learn a great deal from them about life and how it should be lived. In his fantastic tale "Dukh veka" ("The Spirit of the Age," 1900), he writes that men's sufferings stem from the fact that they are becoming increasingly distant from creatures of the animal world. "We have lost their natural beauty," declares his hero, "their grace, strength, and agility, their resilience in the struggle with nature, their vitality" (II, 435). "Emerald" is a moving affirmation of those qualities through the vigorous four year old stallion of the title. The tale's essentials are based on the poisoning of the racehorse "Dawn" by a rival horse breeder as reported in the Moscow papers in the early 1900s. Moreover, as Kuprin's dedication suggests, the literary progenitor of his Emerald was that "incomparable piebald trotter Kholstomer" in Tolstoy's tale of that name.[7] Comparison of the works reveals parallels in treatment and emphasis, but there is an essential difference of technique. While Tolstoy's horse is part man, Kuprin's is all horse. Tolstoy not only endows his horse with human feelings, but gives him the ability to think, using him as a vehicle for social comment and a lens through which to examine the human institution of property. Kuprin's tale, by contrast, is less complex, relying for its power on the visual precision of its description. Choosing not to penetrate his horse's psychology, he relies instead on Emerald's acute sensual awareness of external reality.

That reality is immediate yet ephemeral for the horse, an intriguing but limited universe resting firmly on the triple pillars of

sight, sound, and smell. Indeed, smell is the all-pervasive essence of
this world, and through his animal's receptivity to its infinitely suggestive variety Kuprin paints a delicate picture of a creature at one
with the life around it. Nowhere is this better seen than in Emerald's dream of a pristine morning: "Just before dawn he dreamed
of an early spring morning, a red sunrise over the earth, and a low,
fragrant meadow. The grass was thick and lush, brilliantly, magi-
cally, and delightfully green, and . . . all over it the dew sparkled
with quivering fire. . . . Through the cool of morning he catches the
smell of smoke curling blue and limpid above a chimney in the village, every flower in the meadow has a different scent, on the
damp, rutted road beyond the hedge a multitude of smells are mingled: there is the smell of people and tar and horse dung and dust
and steamy cow's milk from the passing herd, and fragrant resin
from the pine stakes of the fence" (IV, 401). Emerald is the
embodiment of life itself, a gloriously full-blooded creature, exultant in a dazzling world of primary colors and supremely natural
things — "blue sky, green grass, golden sun, miraculous air, the
heady ecstasy of youth, strength, and swift flight" (IV, 402).

But this jubilant hymn to the joy of being ends on a tragic note.
The somber gloom of the closing chapter contrasts starkly with the
triumphant light of Emerald's earlier life. The story's conclusion is
pervaded by an oppressive sense of doom, from the yellow moon
that fills the horse with terror, through the long, empty days of his
captive solitude, to the dancing yellow lantern — that parody of the
sun — which is the last thing he sees. Though it lacks the horror of
Kholstomer's end under the knacker's knife, Emerald's death by
poison is the more moving because of his vibrant youth. His fate is
a tragic illustration of the gulf between the human and the animal
world. Not even the splendid beauty of innocent natural things,
Kuprin infers, is immune to the venality of men.

VIII   *Love Eternal:* Sulamith *and "The Bracelet of Garnets"*

Kuprin could hardly have retreated further from the early 1900s
than to the reign of King Solomon, in which his tale *Sulamith*
(1908) is set. Based closely on *The Song of Songs,* the work tells of
the love between Solomon and Sulamith (Shulamite), the daughter
of a vineyard keeper at Baal-hamon outside Jerusalem. Kuprin had
become interested in *The Song of Songs* many years before, and as
early as 1899 had used part of its third verse — "thy name is as

ointment poured forth" — as the epigraph to his article "Solntse poezii russkoi" ("The Sun of Russian Poetry"), written to mark the centenary of Pushkin's birth.[8] In 1907 his interest in the canticle revived, perhaps as the result of his love for Elizaveta Geinrikh, who in 1909 became his second wife.[9] At one point he described both his fascination with the song of Solomon's love and his reasons for reworking it in prose: "*The Song of Songs* . . . captivates me with the power of its feeling, its poetry, and its lofty, creative inspiration. And I would like this remarkable work of art to become the property of many readers who do not know it at all."[10]

While *The Song of Songs* provides only the faintest idea of its historical context, Kuprin's *Sulamith* sets forth the background of the canticle in infinite detail. Simple enough in itself, his love story is part of a complex historical tableau that breathes oriental exoticism. Feeling that the magnificence of Solomon's life was rivaled only by tales from the *Arabian Nights,* Kuprin creates an ornate picture of biblical antiquity. His erudition is amazing. Drawing on the experience of Flaubert (*Hérodias, Salammbô,* and *La Tentation de Saint Antoine*) and perhaps of Gautier (*La Chaîne d'Or* and *Le Roman de la Momie*), he resurrects the age of Solomon in all its gorgeous color and bejewelled splendor. Whole chapters of *Sulamith* — which Kuprin described as "half historical poem, half legend"[11] — are devoted to a re-creation of antique atmosphere and setting. Thus Chapter I tells in exhaustive detail of the building of the temple of Jerusalem and of the thousands of workmen and materials involved, and Chapter II speaks of Solomon's boundless power and the catholicity of his tastes. While Chapter III reveals his profound learning and Chapter V his wisdom as a judge, Chapters X and XI describe the ecstatic ritual of phallic sacrifice in the temple of Osiris and Isis. But perhaps the most remarkable chapter of all is VIII, in which Solomon explains to his beloved the secret properties of precious stones. These pages illustrate Kuprin's detailed research for his tale: the short chapter encapsulates the exoticism of that legendary time, as it moves from the sapphire of chastity to the moonstone of prophecy, and from the amethyst, which protects its wearer from intoxication, to the emerald, Solomon's favorite, which guards against snakes and scorpions.

Yet for all their scrupulous detail, Kuprin's extensive descriptions are only the decorative frame into which his simple love story is set. All the splendor of Solomon's reign is — in the words of Ecclesiastes — only a "vanity of vanities" beside the love of Sulamith, "a devoted and beautiful love that is more precious than wealth, glory, and wisdom, more precious than life itself..." (IV, 14). Kuprin amplifies the Song of Solomon into the story of the love between the king of Israel and Sulamith, from its chance beginning in a vineyard to its tragic end in the palace, when the girl is stabbed. Skillfully incorporating lines and motifs from *The Song of Songs,* Kuprin sings a lyrical prose hymn to the immortal love of two human beings. Love is the only reality to endure through the ages, for, as the canticle says, it alone is as strong as death. The inspiration and embodiment of that love is the delightful, dark-skinned Sulamith, that "fairest among women," whose matchless but ingenuous beauty mirrors the purity and selflessness of her soul. Despite its idealized quality, this extraordinary love between a king and a poor vine-grower's daughter is untouched by ethereal chill. Solomon and Sulamith are supremely sensual creatures, whose passion leads readily to the triumphant gratification of natural desire. Yet with great delicacy, Kuprin avoids describing their sensuality in overt terms, preferring instead to suggest it subtly through word, gesture, and the seductive atmosphere of their nuptial chamber.

Sulamith is not without its faults. Its excess of historical detail tends to submerge the love story at its center and to retard the narrative. Kuprin's imitation of ponderous biblical rhythm and refrain burdens his prose, and his technique of incorporating lines from the canticle in the speech of Solomon and Sulamith lends their dialogue a stylized quality. Gorky most uncharitably condemned the work as an unnecessary experiment: "Kuprin ... had no need whatsoever to touch *The Song of Songs* — it's fine without his doing anything to it. And anyway, his Solomon resembles a drayman."[12] The Symbolist critic Zinaida Hippius was rather more kind. Though she considered *Sulamith* a "coarse work, a primitive crayon sketch unworthy of Kuprin's talent," she added that she liked it nonetheless, "because of its doubly exotic nature, both Russian and oriental."[13]

Like her predecessor, the less intensely poeticized Olesya, Kuprin's Sulamith is the bearer of her author's idea. She is the embodiment of the rare love that so few ever know. Her tragic end is an eloquent demonstration of her love, for she sacrifices her own life to shield her beloved from the assassin's sword. "All things pass," affirms the inscription on Solomon's ancient ring; but the memory of Sulamith's selfless love echoes down the centuries, immortalized in the canticle to which Kuprin paid a humble prose tribute.

In his strongly autobiographical tale "Lenochka" (1910), Kuprin turned to the love of ordinary mortals in an everyday world where time takes its relentless toll. With Chekhovian restraint he tells of the love of two young people, recalled in the twilight of middle age. His hero Voznitsyn meets his adolescent sweetheart Lenochka on a Crimean steamer, and their chance encounter evokes a sadly poetic recollection of the first stirrings of sensuality thirty years before. Pervaded though it is by wistful melancholy, the tale is quietly optimistic, for it affirms the continuity of life. All things change in a world where life is followed by death, but all our lives are interwoven because life itself never dies. Painfully aware of the proximity of old age, Voznitsyn is fortified by the knowledge that he too has his minuscule place in life's scheme of things. "Life is wise . . . life is beautiful," he explains to Lenochka. "It is an everlasting resurrection from the dead. You and I will leave life . . . but from our minds, inspiration and talent will rise . . . a new Lenochka and a new Kolya Voznitsyn. . . . We all live together . . . both in death and resurrection" (V, 203). Its delicate evocation of the feelings of youth and its elegiac nostalgia for the joys of an irrevocable past make "Lenochka" one of Kuprin's most masterful tales of love.

To Kuprin sadness and tragedy are as much a part of love as the joy and ecstasy it brings to fortunate human beings. The theme of suffering and disappointment in love, already apparent in *Moloch* and *The Duel,* reaches a profoundly moving crescendo in his shorter works of these years. While *Sulamith* speaks of the fulfillment of mutual love, "Telegrafist" ("The Telegraphist," 1911) tells of the loneliness of failure. The sensitive hunchback Vrublevsky has known two loves in his twenty-six years. While the first failed because it was unrequited, the second — a deep, mutual love — was renounced by Vrublevsky himself because he felt ashamed of his physical disability beside the slender elegance of his beloved. Though in only six months his sweetheart married another, there is no bitterness in his generous soul, and with sad resignation he wishes her happiness. She gave him at least the illusion of love, and for that he will always be grateful, "because there is nothing more sacred and beautiful in the world than a woman's love" (V, 331).

The hopelessness of unrequited love holds a special fascination for several of Kuprin's characters, notably Nazansky, who speaks of its delightful torments to Romashov. In the famous story "The

Bracelet of Garnets," (1911), hopeless love finds its quietly tragic apotheosis. Though it develops the theme of unsuccessful love found in "The Telegraphist," the tale pivots on two ideas central to *Sulamith:* that love is as powerful as death, and that real love comes only once in a thousand years. Based on people of Kuprin's acquaintance,[14] the tale has as its main character the timid clerk Zheltkov, a "little man" very like Vrublevsky, who is possessed by a consuming love for Princess Vera Sheina, a rich society lady hardly aware of his existence. Precisely because it is so hopeless, Zheltkov's love lacks the urgent sensuality of *Sulamith.* Instead it is an emotion of boundless nobility and pure selflessness, the highest spiritual experience attainable by man. Kuprin was aware that its purity distinguished Zheltkov's passion from that of other characters in his work: "I'll say one thing," he told Batyushkov, "I've never written anything more chaste."[15]

The structure of "The Bracelet" underlines the hopelessness of Zheltkov's love by revealing the social gulf between him and the princess. The first nine chapters of the thirteen are devoted to a portrayal of her wealthy household, its aristocratic visitors, and the attitudes typical of their social stratum. Indeed, it might be said that Kuprin pays excessive attention to Vera's milieu at Zheltkov's expense, for three-quarters of the tale is told before we meet him in Chapter X, and since he commits suicide shortly afterward, he is alive in only that scene. But the early sections of the work are important for other reasons. The first chapter creates an atmosphere of foreboding with its thick fog, the incessant wailing of the siren, and the storm that casts up the bodies of fishermen on the Black Sea coast. Then an abrupt change in the weather brings the quiet, cloudless days of an unexpectedly warm September. The contrasting weather perhaps foreshadows in allegorical terms Zheltkov's emotional tumult and the welcome peace brought by suicide. But the eventual tragic denouement is more clearly suggested through old General Anosov. A deeply sympathetic creation, he is the most important figure in the princess's circle because he is the mouthpiece for Kuprin's views on love. During a discourse on women and marriage in Chapter VIII, he asks Vera whether every woman does not dream of "a love that is unique, all-forgiving, prepared for anything, humble, and selfless" (V, 256). He then speaks of Vera's secret admirer, who has sent her a gift of blood-red garnets. "Perhaps your life's road has been crossed," he conjectures, "by just such a love of which women dream and of which men are no longer capable" (V, 257). Unlike Vera's husband whose inaccurate parody of Zheltkov's letters points up his own insensitivity, Anosov has detected the truth.

Zheltkov's tragedy is that of a man wholly committed to a single ideal. Compelled by her relatives to cease all communication with the princess, yet certain he can never stop loving her, he can only kill himself. "Nothing interests me in life," he writes to her in his suicide letter, "neither politics, science, philosophy, nor concern for the future happiness of mankind — for me my whole life consists only in you" (V, 266). But neither Zheltkov's living nor his passing are in vain, for his love has found its way into his beloved's heart and brings about her spiritual resurrection. As she looks upon Zheltkov's corpse, Vera recalls Anosov's prophetic words and realizes that the rare, great love of which every woman dreams has passed her by. The cool aristocrat has suddenly become a woman deeply moved by the exceptional love bestowed on her. In a finale unequalled in his writing for its poetic power, Kuprin shows the rebirth of his heroine as she becomes one in spirit with him who loved her more than life itself. As she listens to the mournful largo appassionato of Beethoven's Second Piano Sonata, mentioned in Zheltkov's last letter, the princess hears prose stanzas form to the music in her mind, as if Zheltkov himself is speaking to her. With its refrain of "Blessed be Thy name," his prose poem seems to forgive her for recognizing too late the greatness of his love. "Think of me," he whispers to his grieving beloved as the last notes of the sonata die away, "and I shall be with you, because you and I loved each other only for an instant, and yet forever" (V, 271).

IX   The Lestrigons

The *joie de vivre* that pulses so vigorously in tales like "Emerald" and *Sulamith* reaches its zenith in *Listrigony* (*The Lestrigons,* 1907-11), Kuprin's cycle of sketches about the fishermen of Balaklava. During his visits to the Crimea in the early 1900s, he grew to know the people of Balaklava intimately, learning to fish with them and coming to love the robust simplicity of their life. Set in remote Balaklava, "that most original corner of the motley Russian empire" (V, 278), these eight sketches are a lyrical paean to the simple life and an epic glorification of the sterling virtues of its simple folk. To Kuprin the peaceful life of Balaklava serves as a spiritual tonic for the torpor of civilization. His splendid fishermen embody all the qualities he finds lacking in the life around him. Named after the race of Sicilian giants in Homer's *Odyssey,* from whom according to local legend they are descended, Kuprin's Lestrigons affirm the heroic principle of which he so approved. Bounded only by sea and sky, their free existence demonstrates the superiority of natural man over his civilized fellow. Like that of Jack London's heroes, whom Kuprin so admired, their life is "a noble protest against the closeness, sourness, egoism, timorousness, and limpness of capital cities" (IX, 155). The inhabitants of those cities, the holiday visitors (*dachniki*) to Balaklava, incur Kuprin's contempt in his very first paragraph, as they leave at the end of summer, "with their ... scrofulous children and decadent spinsters" (V, 278).

The wild environment of Balaklava makes the Lestrigons what they are. Their age-long struggle to wrest a livelihood from the sea has forged among them links of friendship that bring exemplary solidarity to their collective. Physical strength and spiritual beauty, unfailing vigor and resolute courage, carefree simplicity and life-asserting spontaneity — these traits delight Kuprin in his toilers of the sea, precious qualities summed up in the lyrical tribute beginning the sixth sketch, "Bora": "Oh, dear, simple people, courageous hearts, ingenuous, primitive souls, strong bodies weathered by the salt sea wind, calloused hands, and sharp eyes that have looked so often into the face of death..." (V, 296). Proud of his friendship with these people and grateful to have been admitted to their rare community, Kuprin describes their life with reverential admiration. All the sketches but VII, "Vodolazy" ("The Divers"), explore the enclosed world of Balaklava from the author's privileged position inside it, and his joy at living in that world gives his *Lestrigons* its vivid immediacy. Whether afloat or ashore, fighting the elements or dancing in revelry, his fishermen assert the exhilaration of living a life that is a priceless gift to man. No dominant hero moves from one sketch to the next, because together they demonstrate the solidarity of a community united by its centuries-old preoccupations and pervaded by the "feeling of intimate comradeship" (V, 299) that Kuprin so prized. Instead we find several characters — Yura Paratino, Kolya Konstandi, Vanya Andrutsaki, and others — who are renowned in different ways. Yura exhibits to the highest degree that astonishing "indifference of the sea fisherman to the unjust blows of fate" traditional among his people. The courage and skill of this simple man mean infinitely more to Kuprin

than the traditional distinctions of the high and mighty of this
world. Yura is not "the German emperor, a famous bass, or a
fashionable writer," he remarks mockingly, "but when I think
what authority and respect surround his name along all the Black
Sea coast, I recall his friendship ... with pleasure and pride"
(V, 281).

The epic quality of *The Lestrigons* springs from Kuprin's fusion
of present and past in his narrative. His fishermen are steeped in
history yet almost untouched by time, for now, in the 1900s, their
skill derives directly from their distant ancestors, who fished these
same Crimean waters long before the days of Odysseus. The
romantic aura lent by historical perspective is heightened by
Kuprin's fifth sketch, the apocryphal tale "Gospodnia ryba"
("The Lord's Fish"), with its revelation of the ancient legends still
current in Balaklava. The evocative atmosphere of antiquity surrounding the sketches is reinforced by more precise historical
detail: the fortresses built by the Genoese along the Crimean coast,
and the wreck in Balaklava bay of the British frigate *Black Prince*
during the Crimean War. History lends symmetry to this tale of the
living present. Echoing the first sketch "Tishina" ("Silence"), with
its mention of Homer's Lestrigons, the last sketch "Beshenoe
vino" ("Furious Wine"), confirms Balaklava and her people in the
timelessness of antiquity. Reflecting on the Balaklavan tradition of
drinking the local wine in early autumn, Kuprin recalls that "on
these same hills three, four, or perhaps five thousand years ago, ...
all the people would celebrate the magnificent feast of Bacchus"
(V, 317). Unchanging in their natural simplicity, his Lestrigons
seem as immortal as the figures of Homeric legend, or the mighty
sea to which they owe their being.

X   *Rural Gloom and Philosophical Despondency*

Though Kuprin's work around 1910 is primarily optimistic,
skepticism and gloom are not wholly absent from his writing of
that time. Such somber notes sound most often when he examines
crucial social issues or speculates on fate and destiny, a subject that
never ceased to fascinate him.

Two important tales of this period reflect his concern at the gulf
between the intelligentsia and people in rural Russia. Set in a
remote village, "Meliuzga" ("Small Fry," 1907) depicts the appalling life of the peasantry, and through its two central characters

illustrates two different views of the people held by the intelligentsia at the time. Surrounded by an ocean of snow deep in the Russian winter, the village teacher, Astrein, and the medical assistant, Smirnov, engage in endless arguments about the peasantry. Astrein is an ineffective Chekhovian figure who believes that one day the whole of life will be transformed into something beautiful. The people too, he thinks, live in expectation of wondrous events, and only a miracle can wake them from their sleep. To him the people are still exactly as they were centuries ago, a dark mass without identity living in ignorance and filth across the silent vastness of Russia. Despite what many say, it is impossible to understand the soul of this people, for it is "as unfathomable as the soul of a cow" (IV, 419).

Exactly where Kuprin stands here is hard to say. While he rejects Smirnov's crude cynicism ("To hell with the future of mankind! May it croak from syphilis and degeneration!" [IV, 428]), he clearly has little sympathy for Astrein's flabby naiveté, despite his good intentions. Nevertheless, Kuprin's final verdict on his characters is clear. His provincial "small fry" not only fail to understand the peasants around them, but cannot comprehend the urgent necessity of doing so in the early 1900s, when social change in Russia seems inevitable. Their end is as pointless as their interminable arguments. After the seemingly endless winter, Astrein finds his longed-for miracle with the advent of spring. But ironically, regeneration in the natural world brings retribution to both men for their spiritual bankruptcy. In the clearly symbolic closing scene they are swept to their deaths by a river in furious spate, that invincible river of life which in the fullness of time bears all before it.

Less somber than its predecessor, "Poprygun'ia-strekoza" ("The Jumping Dragonfly," 1910) is a neater piece that reveals the gap between intelligentsia and people in disturbing terms. Set like "Small Fry" in the wintry wastes of rural Russia, it brings three members of the intelligentsia — a painter (the narrator), a poet, and a musician — face to face with the peasantry when they attend a Christmas concert at the village school. The best number in the program is the children's enactment of Krylov's fable "Strekoza i muravei" ("The Dragonfly and the Ant"), which stresses the value of industry and foresight. In it a dragonfly asks an ant to feed and warm him till the spring, but on hearing that all the dragonfly has done all summer is sing, the ant refuses to help him, saying "Go on then, dance!'' Listening to this rejoinder, the narrator feels that he and his friends are like the improvident dragonfly, and that the eyes of Russia's 150 million peasants are upon them. What links them and his intellectual fellows, he asks himself, with this, ''the greatest, most mysterious and oppressed people on earth''? (V, 221). The answer is nothing, ''neither language, faith, labor, nor art.'' And what reply, he wonders, will he and those like him give on the dread day of reckoning to this people that is both ''child and wild beast, sage and animal''? Like the dragonfly, they can only answer that they have spent their time singing, whereupon the people will respond with the words of the ant. Though God alone knows the destiny of Russia, it seems to Kuprin's narrator that the ant's words are an irrevocable death sentence pronounced on him and his kind.

The gloom of ''Small Fry'' is distilled with disturbing intensity in Kuprin's skeptical tales of this time that explore the mysteries of destiny and fate. The allegorical ''Lavry'' (''Laurels,'' 1909) emphasizes the impermanence of earthly beauty and the transience of fame. Though all things pass and then are repeated in the process of renewal, man finds little consolation in the knowledge that life will continue after he is gone. ''O pudele'' (''About my Poodle'') of the same year reveals that its author is as mystified by life as his dog. What is the point of his brief existence, he asks, and why is it poisoned by suffering? Enveloped in the wintry murk of a Petersburg night, ''V tramvae'' (''In the Tram,'' 1910) is a more despondent tale. To its narrator our planet resembles a tram hurtling into eternity. Its invisible driver is Time, its conductor Death. Human life is as short as a tram ride, and when his time comes each passenger must step off into the darkness. ''Iskushenie'' (''Temptation,'' 1910) is the most sinister of these tales. Its philosophizing narrator believes man is ruled by a terrible law of chance woven into the pattern of life. That law is embodied in a mysterious Someone or Something that is stronger than destiny and controls our lives with an absurd logic of its own. This spirit is malevolent and ironic, and when tempted by man's blind faith in the morrow, it can destroy him in an instant. Its capriciousness is illustrated by the death of an engineer returning to Petersburg after five years in the Far East, who tempts fate with his impatient love for his family and his unthinking certainty of meeting them. As the train pulls into the station, he slips and is crushed before his wife's eyes. It seems to the narrator that this apparently unjust death is an example of the same logic applied by the evil Someone who rules our lives. For who knows what the morrow would have brought the couple — disenchantment, boredom, or even hatred perhaps?

XI   The Pit

Kuprin's novelistic study of prostitution, *The Pit,* was the longest and most ambitious work of his career. Begun in 1908, its first part appeared in 1909, its second in 1914, and its third in 1915. Kuprin began to collect material on prostitution in Kiev in the 1890s, and used it in his tale "Natashka" (1897), which he reworked as "Po-semeinomu" ("In Family Style") while writing Part II of *The Pit.* Though its opening sentence sets the novel "on the furthest outskirts of a large southern town" (VI, 150), its location is any Russian city, as Kuprin remarked: "*The Pit* is Odessa and Petersburg and Kiev."[16] The problem of prostitution became more acute in Russia in the late 1800s and early 1900s because of the growth of urban population caused by industrial expansion. Public concern was reflected in the First All-Russian Congress to combat prostitution, which met in Petersburg in 1910. Kuprin felt strongly on this question. "Prostitution," he once said, "is an even more terrible phenomenon than war or plague."[17] When Part I of his novel appeared, it enjoyed an instant *succès de scandale,* provoking controversy as widespread as that produced by *The Duel* four years before. Though the dominant reaction was one of censure, several eminent critics praised the novel. Alexander Izmaylov, for example, called it an immensely powerful work of a kind not seen since Tolstoy's "Kreutzer Sonata."[18] But with the appearance of Parts II and III six years later it became clear that as a work of literature *The Pit* was far inferior to *The Duel.*

Many weaknesses of the novel stem from the fact that it took seven years to write and that Kuprin became tired of it, finding the completion of Parts II and III difficult and even loathsome. His dislike for the work was intensified by the sensation caused by Part I and by the publication of his own "ending" of *The Pit* by a Petersburg plagiarist in 1913.[19] Kuprin's sporadic work on the novel is reflected in its structure. Its three parts are linked by the flimsiest of transitions, and Part II contains a long section (Chapters II to V) on the procurer Horizon that is of minimal relevance to the plot. While some symmetry is achieved by the rise and fall of the Yama red light district with which the work opens and closes, its action is set artificially in a three month period between those processes and relies on a series of loosely connected episodes (some reminiscent of his sketches of the 1890s) that bear little relation to the theme of prostitution. Moreover, such plot as the novel possesses lacks a clear thread, and too often wanders into digression and superfluous detail. Consequently the work is long and cumbersome, and fails to show Kuprin's purpose clearly. The reader feels that *The Pit* outgrew its author's initial intentions and swamped them. From a necessary, topical study of prostitution it swelled into a vast, disordered canvas depicting the social and moral issues of its age, many of which are only tenuously linked with the problem of vice. Somehow Kuprin manages to introduce them all: ignorance, inequality, the depravity of Russian society, the relationship between intelligentsia and people, philanthropy and liberalism, socialism and anarchy, revolution and pogroms, art and its restorative power, education, environment, and the unexpectedly relevant question of the economic pressures that give rise to prostitution. The weight of this material rests precariously on the slender pillars of a handful of episodes in the lives of the whores in Kuprin's brothel. Four such episodes are Likhonin's attempts to "save" the prostitute Lyubka, and the visit to the brothel by the actress Rovinskaya (Part II); and the shorter scenes involving the cadet Gladyshev and Zhenka, and the thief Senka and Tamara (Part III).

Kuprin could not decide whether his novel should be documentary reportage or pure fiction, and either oscillates between the two or attempts to combine them in an artificial way. But he is more successful when in documentary vein, and so Part I, with its details of life in the brothel, is by far the best. Though not maintained throughout, this documentary technique was clearly central to his initial didactic purpose in writing *The Pit,* a purpose suggested by his epigraph to the novel: "I know many will find this tale immoral and improper, but nevertheless ... I dedicate it to *mothers* and *young people*" (VI, 150). On the instructive aim of the work he wrote: "I only attempted to throw correct light on the life of prostitutes and to show they should not be regarded as they have been hitherto."[20] But Kuprin's documentation of brothel life is not infrequently overdone, and burdens his narrative. Perhaps the best example of this occurs in Chapter XV of Part II, where during Likhonin's visit to Anna Markovna's establishment to collect Lyubka's papers, Kuprin first provides exhaustive details of the girl's income and expenses as a whore, then enumerates the official rules concerning the hygiene and conduct of prostitutes. *The Pit* employs Kuprin's familiar device of a pair of characters — one older and more experienced — who discuss issues central to the work and arrive at conclusions that reflect their creator's views. Here the student Likhonin and the reporter Platonov are descendants of Bobrov-Goldberg and Romashov-Nazansky. But there is an essential difference between *The Pit* and the long prose works that preceded it. While in *Moloch* and *The Duel* Bobrov and Romashov were set in the center of the stage, here neither Likhonin nor Platonov is a central character. Kuprin is interested not so much in the psychology of individual characters as in the life of a particular social group — his prostitutes and those associated with them. This lack of personal focus makes *The Pit* very unsatisfying artistically, however convincing it may be as a social document. What human interest the work possesses is either blanketed by Kuprin's plethora of subsidiary themes or submerged by his documentary preoccupations.

Platonov is Kuprin's mouthpiece in the novel. A wooden figure who plays no essential part in the work, he is a *raisonneur* who stands on the periphery of the action, obediently commenting on it for Kuprin. His position as an intimate observer of brothel life is oddly equivocal, and his relationship with the various prostitutes curiously avuncular. After helping his author explain the bases, workings, and effects of prostitution, he drifts out of the novel as mysteriously as he first appeared, a lifeless assemblage of weighty words. The core of his tiresome philosophizing is that the horror of prostitution lies precisely in the fact that those engaged in it see nothing horrible about it. What is terrible is not the trade in female flesh, but "the everyday, accustomed trivialities, these daily, commercial, businesslike calculations, ... this matter-of-fact practice laid down over the centuries" (VI, 204). But Platonov's (and evidently Kuprin's) views on prostitution are somewhat confused. Asked by Likhonin when prostitution will cease, he replies naively: "Perhaps when the beautiful Utopias of the socialists and anarchists come true, ... when love is absolutely free" (VI, 233). But while marriage exists, he goes on, prostitution will survive, maintained by the so-called "decent people" in society. Then he argues that man is a polygamous animal whose instincts urge him to enjoy many women, a view which implies that prostitution will last forever and that social factors have little to do with it.

Other characters are hardly more convincing than Platonov.

Likhonin is an insubstantial figure who voices Kuprin's belief that attempts by members of the upper classes to rescue "fallen women" are doomed to fail, and that a more radical solution to the problem of prostitution is needed — though he does not say what. The actress Rovinskaya and the lawyer Ryazanov are, as one Soviet critic points out,[21] episodic characters portrayed in a romantic manner reminiscent of Kuprin's earliest tales. While Rovinskaya has "long, green, Egyptian eyes and ... a red, sensual mouth" (VI, 264), Ryazanov is "tall, ... with a broad forehead like Beethoven's ... and the appearance of a ladykiller" (VI, 416). Except for Lyubka and Zhenka, the fifteen prostitutes in the novel are static creatures. During her association with Likhonin, Lyubka displays unsuspected qualities of sincerity and devotion, while Zhenka, realizing she has syphilis, is consumed by a vengeful desire to infect as many men as possible before she dies. Paradoxically, Kuprin is more effective when portraying minor characters — the brothel proprietress Anna Markovna, her housekeeper Emma Eduardovna, and the local policeman Kerbesh.

The Pit is not one of Kuprin's best works, as he himself admitted in a letter of 1918: "The tale turned out pale, crumpled, untidy, and cold, and was in all fairness torn to pieces by the critics. Serves it right!"[22] Not only did he lack a clear objective in writing the novel, but also had no solution for the problem of prostitution it examined. To a reader who wrote asking what could be done, he could only reply as Platonov did to Zhenka when she turned to him for advice: "I don't know!" (VI, 391). The postscript to his letter revealed his sense of failure in a work to which he had devoted so much time and energy: "I'm not fit to be a teacher of life: I've ruined all my own life as far as it's possible."[23] As a study of prostitution The Pit is unique, but as literature it leaves much to be desired. It was to be Kuprin's last major work, and to many it signaled the decline of his creativity.

CHAPTER 6

War and Revolution

MUCH of Kuprin's work between 1912 and the outbreak of the First World War is inferior. Inconsequential in its subjects, it simply restates themes from his earlier writing. Several tales of these years turn on his memories of the past — "Travka" ("Little Grass," 1912), "V medvezh'em uglu" ("In a God-Forsaken Place"), and "A White Lie" (1914). Others are humorous pieces of an anecdotal kind, such as "Svetlyi konets" ("A Bright End,"1913) and "Vinnaia bochka" ("The Wine Barrel," 1914). Perhaps most successful are his animal tales for children, among them "Medvedi" ("The Bears," 1912), "Ezh" ("The Hedgehog," 1913), and "Brikki" ("Bricky," 1914). However, three works of this time are sufficiently significant to deserve special mention. While the tales "Black Lightning" and "Anathema" continue the theme of protest found in earlier works, the travel sketches *The Côte d'Azur* show Kuprin's abiding thirst for new experience.

I *"Black Lightning" and "Anathema"*

"Chernaia molniia" ("Black Lightning," 1912) is a powerful indictment of provincial inertia reminiscent of "Small Fry." The work falls into three distinct sections. Its introductory pages describe a northern town so remote that even the worst traveling circuses pass it by. Moribund and undistinguished, it is a cultural and spiritual vacuum, cut off from the world by mud in summer and snow in winter. The center of the tale is a satirical portrayal of the local "intelligentsia," who epitomize the philistinism of provincial life. Sunk in mediocrity and pettiness, they are interested in nothing, and their vegetative existence is enlivened only by drink, cards, and gossip. The third part of the story examines a progressive character whose passionate ideals show up the spiritual bank-ruptcy of his fellow provincials. For the solitary forester Tur-chenko, the forest is his consuming love. Like Astrov in Chekhov's *Uncle Vanya,* his fanatical devotion to his ideal has earned him the reputation of a crank. To him the forest is one of man's most pre-cious resources, and properly utilized it can transform the face of Russia. But he must struggle constantly against the apathy of the authorities and the greed of the peasants, who plunder the forest at will. The lethargy of provincial life is to blame, he believes, for in its stagnation it holds nothing dear. "All around is triviality," he tells the narrator, "all have grown short of intellect, feeling, even simple human words..." (V, 372).

The significance of the work's title only becomes clear toward the end. The image of black lightning is taken from Gorky's prose poem "The Song of the Stormy Petrel" (1901), which hailed the petrel as the herald of the tempest, a symbolic allusion to the com-ing revolutionary storm. During the social evening at the center of Kuprin's tale, the Justice of the Peace ridicules Gorky's words "The petrel flies like black lightning" as sheer nonsense. But as his later account to the narrator reveals, Turchenko has actually seen black lightning with his own eyes, a blinding flash accompanied by a clap of thunder that flung him to the ground. The symbolism of Kuprin's lightning as a destructive revolutionary force that will confound those who have no faith in it, is made clearer by Tur-chenko's words at the close, when he says provincial life is a fetid swamp, and the flash of black lightning upon it is long overdue.

"Anathema" is a much denser work, in which Kuprin aims his protest at the hypocrisy of the Church. Understandably, Tolstoy is the moving force of the tale. His story "Kazaki" ("The Cossacks") was Kuprin's favorite work, one he read dozens of times. "Here it is," he wrote of the tale in 1910, "true beauty, precision, grandeur, humor, spirit, radiance."[1] Two years earlier he had voiced his indig-nation at the hypocrisy of Tolstoy's eighty-year jubilee in 1908. "What kind of a jubilee is it for a writer," he wrote, "in a country where he is excommunicated from the Church and where ... from the pulpit vulgar oaths are heaped upon him!"[2] The strange sight of a volume of Tolstoy in the house of the archdeacon of Gatchina provided the stimulus for Kuprin's tale.

The life-affirming power of "The Cossacks" is responsible for the spiritual transformation of Father Olympus and his decision to leave the Church. His triple reading of it has convinced him that he should have been "a hunter, warrior, fisherman, or ploughman, but never an ecclesiastic" (V, 456). When instructed to anathematize Tolstoy from his pulpit, he remembers the insistent words of the tale "God has created everything for man's joy" (V, 460), and feels he cannot curse a man whose writing has made him weep with gladness. So he booms out the blessing "Long life!" and the choir joyfully takes up his words, filling the church with sound.

The tale is a subtle blend of humor, irony, and straightforward description that shows Kuprin's versatility at its best. His changes of key skillfully bring the drama of the work to a jubilant crescendo as Olympus refuses to execrate Tolstoy. The humor of the opening scene, when the priest tries his voice, gives way to the solemnity of the Creed and the categorical curses. But from the moment Olympus is asked to anathematize Tolstoy, Kuprin begins to interweave in his hero's mind passages from "The Cossacks" with the order of service, in a bizarre verbal duel ending with the victory of Tolstoy. Olympus's exit from the cathedral is a moment of supreme majesty. Removing his vestments and kissing his stole in farewell, he walks through the church, "towering head and shoulders above the people, . . . and the congregation . . . parted before him, forming a wide path" (V, 461–62). The closing lines achieve the symmetry of which Kuprin was so fond, as in a brief scene balancing the beginning of the tale, Olympus is confronted by his anonymous, nagging wife. But filled with the strength of self-awareness Tolstoy's tale has given him, he challenges her angrily and for the first time in her life she falls timidly silent, while her husband walks on, "immensely huge, dark, and majestic, like a monument" (V, 462). Polished, compact, subtly charged with emotion, "Anathema" is one of Kuprin's best tales.

II The Côte d'Azur

Kuprin's visit to the South of France between April and July 1912 gave rise to *Lazurnye berega (The Côte d'Azur),* a cycle of travel impressions. Begun in May of 1912, the twenty sketches were completed in 1913 after his return to Russia. This first journey abroad took him briefly to many places in southern Europe. Passing through Austria and Switzerland, he stayed in Nice and Marseille before visiting Genoa, Venice, Livorno, and Corsica. Highly varied in content, the sketches range from his directions for tourists abroad (I) and an open air performance of Bizet's *Carmen* in

Fréjus (IX), to a description of the Corsican town of Bastia (XIV), and the elusiveness of the Russian consul in Marseille (XIX). But it was not Kuprin's aim to offer a Baedeker-like account of the places he visited. Indeed, as his words in sketch XVI suggest, such traditional guides provide no information on the things that interest him most: "...I am attracted neither by museums, galleries, ... nor theatres, but three places always draw me irresistibly: a little bar, ... a big harbor, and in the heat of the day a cool, old, half-dark church when there is no one there..." (VI, 68). Though his words should not be taken literally (the sketch "Venice" voices his wonder at the beauty of St. Mark's), their essence is true. What most interests him is the everyday life of ordinary folk and the atmosphere of their environment. Only through close contact with them, he believes, can one come to know the temperament of a foreign people. Such contact was soon achieved, as the correspondent of the Petersburg *Birzhevye vedomosti (Stock-Exchange Gazette)* wrote while Kuprin was in Nice: "he has quickly got on friendly terms with local fishermen, syndicates of cabbies, drivers, and workmen of various kinds...."[3] Of his visit to Marseille Kuprin himself said: "What interested me most was to come in contact with the street.... I would spend whole days .... among all those porters, vendors, sailors, and workmen of every kind, and their womenfolk."[4]

On the other hand, Kuprin was revolted by the tinsel artificiality of the Riviera, with its sordid diversions, its venality and hypocrisy. Nice he describes as "a vast human misunderstanding" (VI, 13), a sprawling international hotel built by snobbish Englishmen, aping Russians, rich Americans, and obsequious French. Monte Carlo fares no better under his pen. A den of gamblers and thieves, it poisons the whole Côte d'Azur. On closer inspection, Kuprin continues in disgust, it seems to the visitor that he is in "some place infected with plague and stricken by an epidemic" (VI, 21). But Marseille evokes his passionate admiration, and to it he devotes four sketches (XV–XVIII), describing the city, the port, the old town, and the Château d'If. "I must say," he writes in the first, "never in my life have I seen a more original, lively, and colorful town, that is magnificent and dirty, furiously bustling and quiet, and terribly expensive and cheap at the same time" (VI, 65). But the port of Marseille fascinates him most, and in a detailed sketch that is both documentary and lyrical he speaks of its myriad cargoes, alluring smells, and vessels from all corners of the globe. Venice too intrigues him, but this closing sketch is tinged with sadness at an exquisite but dead city of quiet canals and coffinlike gondolas. "Beautiful Venice," he writes, "recalls a vast graveyard with dead, uninhabited houses . . . and old churches visited by no one but idle travelers" (VI, 85).

Never does Kuprin forget he is a Russian, and he thinks sadly that here abroad people are more free than they are at home. In Marseille on Bastille Day he feels like an uninvited guest at another's feast and reflects on Russia, whose people have no day to commemorate their past. Yet he longs to return to Russia, despite all her faults. His proud nationalism leads him to an oversimplification in his impressions of foreign lands and people. "Apart from the dear, hospitable, . . . cheerful Italians," he .concludes summarily, "all Europeans are slaves to habitual gestures, niggardly, cruel, . . . devout when necessary, and patriotic when it pays. . ." (VI, 11). Based on a stay abroad of less than four months, and most of that spent on the untypical French Riviera, the remark reveals as much about Kuprin as about the Europeans to whom it refers.

While in Nice Kuprin received an invitation from Gorky to visit him on Capri. He mentions the occasion in sketch XII, speaking of Gorky as "a certain famous Russian writer . . . whose bright, pure soul I deeply respect" (VI, 48). Gorky's gesture was apparently an attempt to restore relations between the two men, which had cooled since 1905. But eager as Kuprin was at the prospect, the meeting was not to be. He was delayed by a seamen's strike and when the journey became possible, found himself without money. He was saddened by his failure to reach Capri, and on returning to Russia told a reporter it would have been "a great joy to see Gorky," who had invited him with "such a kind, friendly letter."[5]

III   *The War Years: Patriotism and Satire*

The outbreak of the First World War awoke the ardent patriot in Kuprin. In a series of articles and interviews he condemned the Germans as barbarians bent on the annihilation of Russia. "Against us come hordes of savage, uncivilized Huns," he wrote, "who will burn and destroy everything in their path and who must themselves be utterly destroyed."[6] Horrified by the suffering inflicted on defenseless civilians, he saw in these henchmen of Prussian militarism sadistic madmen intoxicated with the blood of innocents. It was the duty of every Russian, he believed, to fight the foe in a war in which Russia was fulfilling God's will. The war with Germany was a war to end wars, a holy crusade by the Russian people to bring liberation to the world and death to war itself.

For all his nationalistic fervor, in no work of these years does Kuprin give a detailed picture of either fighting or military events. The reason was simple. "I do not consider it possible," he explained to a reporter, "to write war stories without having been at the front. . . . I have not been in war, and so the psychology of fighting soldiers is totally alien to me. . . ."[7] Moreover, he openly despised writers who wrote pompously about the war without ever hearing the sound of gunfire. To describe war correctly, he believed, a writer must experience it at first hand, as Tolstoy had.

His first work to reflect the war, however briefly, is the lyrical "Sny" ("Dreams") of October 1914. Discussing various kinds of dreams, Kuprin focuses on the familiar illusion of flying in dreams, and sees in it proof that long ago man's ancestors really did fly. The thought leads him to the bizarre conclusion that the brotherhood of man can only be achieved through "the great art of flying, with its pure, blissful joys and its great freedom" (VI, 145). Though now "the wings of mankind's finest, eternal dream beat convulsively in blood and fire," Kuprin asserts that one day man will fly again, for "he has come into the world for boundless freedom, creation, and happiness." How that freedom allegorized by flight will emerge from the holocaust of war is unclear.

The story "Sad prechistoi devy" ("The Garden of the Most Pure Virgin," 1915) gives a clearer picture of Kuprin's view of the horrors of war. Like the apocryphal tale "Dva sviatitelia" ("The Two Saints") of the same year, it is a popularization of biblical legend. As the Virgin Mary walks through her wondrous garden, she has dread visions of earthly slaughter: ". . . mountains of corpses . . . bleeding wounds, battlefields dark with flocks of carrion crows" (VI, 442). The sins of men have enveloped the earth in a bloody conflagration, and such is God's wrath that even the flowers in the Virgin's paradise garden are filled with bloody dew. Though vivid and powerful, "The Garden" suffers from the same excessive sentimentality found in Kuprin's earlier apocryphal tales and legends.

More effective are his satires on civilians in the rear engaged in speculation and embezzlement. While Russia runs with blood, these despicable creatures safely amass their fortunes. Such are the heroes of the tales "Goga Veselov" and "Kantalupy" ("The Cantaloups") of 1916, both set in Petrograd. The first takes the form of a dream in which the narrator hears the success story of his friend Veselov, once a profligate and now a millionaire. Veselov has used his post in the investigation department to blackmail wealthy people whose compromising letters he secretly opens. He has no qualms in justifying his dishonesty: what is the good, he asks, of living one's whole life honorably only to die like a pig at the end of it? If others spend their lives in enjoyment, why should he not do the same? "Veselov" is a bright tale whose only weakness is that its later pages are encumbered with details of blackmail techniques.

"The Cantaloups" is more polished. Its satire on corrupt bureaucracy was so biting that Kuprin gave it the subtitle "Perhaps a fiction" in an effort to outwit the severe censorship of the war years. Its hero Bakulin, chief clerk in the department of supply, purchase, and transport, takes enormous bribes from the dubious businessmen who visit his office. In a short time he has many possessions, including two townhouses and a dacha. This unctuous hypocrite resembles Nasedkin of "A Quiet Life" as he feigns indignation at an awkwardly proffered bribe — "What? A bribe? Who for? Me? At a time like this?" (VII, 86) — or bemoans the fate of "poor, long-suffering Russia gasping in the clutches of bribetakers, embezzlers, . . . and scoundrels" (VII, 88). The loving father of his family, Bakulin finds respite from the pressures of daily extortion in the quiet cultivation of his melons with his seductive sister-in-law. Kuprin's irony is at its most acid in the closing scene. Kneeling in prayer before the icon of St. Nicholas, Bakulin says that all the money he has taken is only for his family and that all his acquisitions are in his wife's name. While others spend to excess, his only amusement is growing melons. If he can amass a million, he will resign his job, devote his life to good works, and perhaps build a church. But here Kuprin informs us that Bakulin has already made well over two million, and that not long before he promised to stop at two hundred thousand. In a final thrust of supreme irony Kuprin shows his hero sound asleep under the gaze of St. Nicholas, "who once interceded for the thief who had stolen a crust of bread for his starving family" (VI, 89).

Satire is the essence of "Papasha" ("Daddy") too, written in 1915. Though Kuprin subtitled the tale "a fable," it was banned and not published till 1916. It is a humorous exposé of the sham liberalism professed by high officials. When a general becomes head of a government department, he benevolently allows his subordinates unheard-of freedom in the execution of their duties. But one day he is struck on the head by a bust of Montesquieu and is transformed into a tyrant who rages at his staff. Intriguingly, Kuprin leaves his reader in doubt as to when the general was mad — before or after his collision with Montesquieu.

In the tale "Grunya" (1916) Kuprin's satire is aimed at falsity in literature. Its hero Gushchin is a successful but ignorant writer, totally divorced from reality and unable to perceive in the life around him the significant details so essential to true art. Like many writers, he sees in war only splendid heroics and melodramatic clichés. After hearing an officer's laconic account of an attack, he concludes condescendingly that the soldier is no artist, since "he remembers only trivia and hasn't grasped the essentials" (VII, 65), a view that is clearly false. Gushchin's paltriness as a human being is emphasized by his terror when faced by Grunya's huge peasant uncle, the epitome of the common folk he affects to know so well. Also indicative of Kuprin's concern at the lamentable condition of writing during the war is the short tale "Interv'iu" ("The Interview," 1916). Describing the visit paid by a correspondent to a playwright, it offers a light-hearted parody of newspaper articles that bear no relation to what was said in the interview from which they derive.

Other tales of the war years are based on people of Kuprin's acquaintance or on personal experience. While "Lyutsiya" ("Lucia," 1916) draws on events of circus life in Kiev in the 1890s, "Gogol'-mogol' " ("Egg Flip." 1915) tells of Shaliapin's first stage appearance, his energy and his talent. "Gad" ("A Vile Creature," 1915) is built around a confession heard by the narrator and recalls "Off the Street." Set in Kiev in 1893, it describes the misadventures of a provincial fortuneteller and includes facts from Kuprin's biography. Several other works are more closely autobiographical. "The Buried Infants" (1915) reflects his stay in Polesye, while "Fialki" ("The Violets," 1915) recalls his first love as a cadet. Akin to it is "Khrabrye begletsy" ("The Gallant Fugitives," 1917), which draws upon his years in the Razumovsky boarding school. Tinged though they are with sentimentality, such tales are sincere in their nostalgia for vanished youth. The same can be said of the sensitive stories about birds and animals that also belong to these years. The lyricism of "Skvortsy" ("Starlings," 1916) and the humor of "Kozlinaia zhizn' " ("A Goat's Life," 1917) stand beside the seriousness of "Mysli Sapsana II" ("The Thoughts of Sapsan II," 1917), in which through a dog Kuprin makes telling observations on people and life.

IV *1917: Political Ambivalence*

The revolution of February 1917 found Kuprin in Helsinki, where he had gone on medical advice. Returning to Gatchina, he expressed his enthusiasm at the collapse of tsarism in a series of articles in several papers. In May he became an editor of the Socialist Revolutionary paper *Svobodnaia Rossiya (Free Russia)*, contributing to it a regular *feuilleton* entitled *Pestraia kniga (The Motley Book)*, before moving in August to the paper *Vol'nost' (Freedom)*. In addition, for much of 1917 he contributed to *Petrogradskii listok (The Petrograd Leaflet)*. But the political persuasion of the papers in which he was published between the revolutions of 1917 in no way reflected his own views. Diversity and even confusion characterize his writing of these months. While welcoming the freedom brought by the February Revolution, he foresaw the excesses that further upheaval might bring and feared lest Russia plunge into an orgy of bloodshed. His journalistic activities left him little time for fiction, and in the interval between the revolutions of 1917 he published only two new works — the sketch "Liudi-ptitsy" ("Bird Men") and the tale "Sashka and Yashka," both of which deal with aviation and contain only a distant reflection of war.

The October Revolution did little to clarify Kuprin's political position. In the articles he contributed to various papers till mid-1918 — including *Petrogradskoe ekho (Petrograd Echo)*, *Vechernee slovo (Evening Word)*, and *Zaria (Dawn)* — his attitude to the new regime remained ambivalent. He recognized the historical significance of the Bolshevik Revolution and admired Lenin as "an absolutely honest and courageous man."[8] Denouncing the assassination of a prominent Bolshevik in July 1918, he wrote: "Bolshevism constitutes a great, pure, disinterested doctrine that is inevitable for mankind."[9] Yet elsewhere he argued that the Bolsheviks threatened Russian culture, and that their insufficient knowledge of the country had brought suffering to her people. In June of 1918, Kuprin was even arrested for a short time for an article in the paper *Molva (Rumor)* critical of the regime.[10] His political ambivalence emerges in two tales of March 1918. "The Caterpillar" is a retrospective work that not only marks the first anniversary of the

February Revolution but also returns to 1905, praising the heroism of women revolutionaries and revealing the role one of them played in rescuing sailors from the *Ochakov*. But "Gatchinskii prizrak" ("The Ghost of Gatchina") is an anti-Bolshevik tale of the horror of civil war and the tyranny of Russia's new masters.[11]

However, late 1918 saw an apparent rapprochement between Kuprin and the new regime, when he drew up elaborate plans for *Zemlia (Land)*, a paper designed specially for the peasantry. His program expressed his intention to assist the government in the radical transformation of rural life along lines not conflicting with the principles of communism. Most ambitious in its aims, *Land* was to cover everything from methods of soil improvement and crop rotation to mechanization and the provision of works of literature for the rural reader. But though supported by Gorky and approved by Lenin himself at a meeting with Kuprin on December 25, 1918, the project was never realized.[12] His renewed association with Gorky involved Kuprin in the *Vsemirnaia literatura (World Literature)* publishing house founded by Gorky in 1918. At Gorky's request, Kuprin wrote a preface for a Russian edition of Dumas père and early in 1919 translated Schiller's *Don Carlos*.[13] Like *Land,* however, neither actually appeared. Apart from this, Kuprin produced little new work in the months before his emigration. While 1918 saw the apocryphal tale "Pegie loshadi" ("Skewbald Horses") and the historical piece "Tsarskii pisar' " ("The Tsar's Clerk"), 1919 saw only "Volshebnyi kayer" ("The Magic Carpet"), probably his last work before his departure.

Despite what his *Land* project suggests, Kuprin was never firmly pro-Bolshevik after 1917, and it is doubtful whether the revolution made him any more of a political animal than he had been before it.[14] His continuing political stance is best described by his assertion after the October Revolution: "I have never belonged to any party, belong to none now, and never shall."[15] The result of circumstance rather than conviction, his emigration did not indicate any fundamental change in his essentially apolitical position.

CHAPTER 7

The Twilight Years

I Emigration

EVEN during his brief stay of 1919–1920 in Finland, Kuprin sensed that the life of an émigré was not for him. The next seventeen years in Paris not only witnessed the decline of his creativity, but eventually broke his spirit. Grieved at his separation from Russia and never truly at home among his fellow émigrés, he became lonely and withdrawn. Though he himself criticized the Bolshevik regime in several articles of the early 1920s, he was annoyed by the rabidly anti-Soviet attitude of many émigrés. In his article "Nansenovskie petukhi" ("Nansen's Cockerels," 1921) he likened them to Nansen's rooster on the *Fram* which, disoriented by the polar darkness, went out of its mind crowing at the sun that refused to rise.[1] The social pressures of émigré circles irked him too. "Living ... in Russian emigration," he wrote, "is like living ... in a crowded room where a dozen bad eggs have been smashed ... we've tasted to excess all the vileness of gossip, bickering, pretense, intrigue, suspicion ... stupidity, and boredom."[2] The family's poverty only made the situation worse. "I'm left naked ... and destitute as a homeless old dog," Kuprin wrote to a friend.[3] But his separation from Russia pained him most, for it hindered his writing. "The more talented a man is," he told a reporter in 1925, "the harder it is for him without Russia."[4]

Kuprin's nostalgia does much to explain the predominantly retrospective quality of his work in emigration. He returns to familiar themes from his earlier writing and dwells on personal experiences linking him with the homeland he has lost. However varied his sixty or so works of these years may be — they range from travel sketches and animal tales to poetry and the film scenario

Rakhil' (Rachel) — they introduce little that is new. Perhaps the most effective are those pervaded by longing for Russia. The distant tsarist past is the basis for several historical works. Thus "Odnorukii komendant" ("The One-Armed Commandant," 1923) tells of the Skobelevs, a military family renowned for its bravery, and "Ten' Napoleona" ("The Shade of Napoleon," 1928) is a humorous account of the absurd attempts by officials in 1912 to locate veterans who had seen Napoleon at Borodino a century before. More interesting is the anecdotal tale "Tsarev gost' iz Narovchata" ("The Tsar's Guest from Narovchat," 1933) which sketches Kuprin's native town and describes the visit paid by a laughable local landowner to Alexander I. Reminiscent of Nikolay Leskov's historical pieces, these tales have an old-fashioned, musty flavor stemming from their archaic vocabulary and unhurried narrative. Akin to them are several fables and legends. The sinister "Skazka" ("Fairy Tale," 1920) was followed by the exotic Eastern legend "Sud'ba" ("Destiny," 1923), first entitled "Kismet," and by the more traditional tale "Siniaia zvezda" ("The Blue Star," 1925), a story of a Utopian land where people never lie. Rather different is "Gero, Leander i pastukh" ("Hero, Leander and the Goatherd," 1929), an irreverent variant of the classical legend in which Kuprin's satyric goatherd seduces Hero as she awaits her beloved. "Skripka Paganini" ("Paganini's Violin") of the same year tells how Paganini sold his soul to the devil and achieved fame, but learned at his death that true art is the gift not of Satan but of God.

Treasured memories of Kuprin's past gave rise to another group of Parisian tales. Such are the hunting stories "Noch' v lesu" ("A Night in the Forest," 1931) and "Val'dshnepy" ("The Woodcock," 1933), both set in Ryazan Province, and "Zaviraika" (1928), subtitled "A Dog's Soul," a recollection of Danilovskoe. Like the latter are Kuprin's many tales about animals and birds — "Bal't" ("Balt," 1929), "Barri" ("Barry," 1931), "Udod" ("The Hoopoe," 1932), and "Zolotoi petukh ("The Golden Cockerel," 1923), one of the best works of his emigration. His own experiences are reflected too in several circus tales in which he recalls performers' courage and skill. Among them are "Doch' velikogo Barnuma" ("Great Barnum's Daughter," 1927), "Olga Sur" (1929), and "Blondel" (1933). Other works are variants or extensions of earlier material relating to Kuprin's past. Thus "Ferdinand" (1930) echoes *Olesya,* "The Swamp," and "Black Lightning" in its enumeration of the extraordinary things seen by Kuprin, while the Balaklavan sketch *"Svetlana"* is a nostalgic post-script to *The Lestrigons* of two decades earlier.

More original are the many sketches that convey Kuprin's impressions of life abroad. His visit to southwest France in 1925 inspired "Puntsovaia krov' " ("Crimson Blood," 1926), a color-ful account of a bullfight in Bayonne and a hymn to the matador's skill. It was followed in 1927 by "Iug blagoslovennyi" ("The Blessed South"), four sketches on Gascony and the Hautes Pyrénées, in which Kuprin admires the vivid beauty of the South with its quaint towns steeped in history and its towering mountains with their countless torrents. Similar but less evocative are the pre-dominantly urban sketches in *Yugoslavia,* the product of Kuprin's visit to Belgrade in 1928 to attend a conference of émigré Russian writers. From Belgrade itself, he turns to Yugoslav hospitality, the beauty of their women, and the details of national dishes. More intriguing are his sketches of Paris. The cycle *Domashnii Parizh (Domestic Paris, 1927),* touches on many features of Parisian life, from the city's vanishing *fiacres* to fishing on the Seine, from the demolition of old taverns to the modernization of Passy, once so full of Russian émigrés. "Parizh intimnyi" ("Intimate Paris," 1930) is a short piece on the family life of Parisians which refutes the notion that French women are immoral.

For all their praise of France and her people, these sketches are tinged with the retrospective sadness characteristic of Kuprin's work in emigration. Nostalgic echoes of Russia sound again and again in these works, reminding their author that he is an alien. While the little town of Auch in Gascony recalls Mogilev-on-Dnieper, its young people out walking in the evening remind him of Kolomna, Ustyuzhna, and Petrozavodsk. Likewise, as he sits on the veranda of a café, Kuprin imagines himself in the garden of a Tiflis *dukhan* (Caucasian tavern). Though majestic, the Pyrenees are not so magnificent as the mountains of the Crimea or the Caucasus. "But ... it's long been well-known," he exclaims, "that everything's better in Russia!" (VII, 350). In *Domestic Paris* he wonders why the city so often reminds him of Moscow, and ascribes this to "painful shades of nostalgia" (VII, 405). Saddest of all is *Mys Guron (Cape Huron, 1929),* a cycle of sketches inspired by Kuprin's visit to Provence that year. Describing fisher-men at work near Le Lavandou, he wistfully recalls his beloved Balaklava, lost now forever in the distant past.

II   *Last Major Works*

Three works of Kuprin's Parisian years deserve special mention — *The Wheel of Time* (1929), *The Junkers* (1932), and *Zhaneta* (*Jeannette,* 1933), all steeped in nostalgia for Russia and the past.

Though styled a novel, *The Wheel of Time* is actually a collection of thirteen sketchlike chapters, seven of which appeared in the Paris paper *La Renaissance* between February and May of 1929. Taken together, they constitute a protracted reminiscence by their Russian narrator Mikhail of his love affair with a beautiful aristocrat in Marseille. *The Wheel of Time* abounds in echoes of Kuprin's earlier work, notably his visit to Marseille in *The Côte d'Azur* and his impressions of Balaklava in *The Lestrigons*. But its central theme stems from *Sulamith* and "The Bracelet of Garnets": a great love that is the rarest of gifts bestowed on man. However, while those works stressed the reciprocity of intense love, either in life or death, *The Wheel of Time* describes a relationship that founders because one partner loves more than the other. Mikhail cannot love Maria with the generosity with which she loves him; sated with her adoring love, he grows complacent, then indifferent, and she leaves him forever. Too late he sees that his dry intellectualism has prevented him from loving her with the spontaneity she deserved. But he submits to fate, he concludes sadly, for the wheel of time can never be turned back. Filled with memories of a vigorous past when happiness was at its zenith, *The Wheel of Time* is an elegiac testimony to its author's sadness at the onset of old age.

The Junkers is more nearly autobiographical. A lengthy personal memoir begun in 1911, it was finally published serially between January 1928 and October 1932 in *La Renaissance.* Intended as a continuation of the autobiographical tale "At the Turning Point," it was designed as a prologue to *The Duel.* Its inordinately long period of composition helps to explain the work's structural flaws. Moreover, its three parts were not written in order. Instead, Part II was written first, followed by Parts I and III, the latter being the least polished of all. This disordered composition produced poor linkages between chapters, confused chronology, repetition, and narrative heaviness. The most glaring inconsistency occurs in Part III, where no reference is made to the hero Alexandrov's love for Zina Belysheva, whom he swore to marry at the close of Part II. Kuprin appears to have completely forgotten this important element of his story, and in Part III simply allows Alexandrov's love to evaporate.

Saddened by the Parisian present, Kuprin retreated gratefully to the Russian past. His *Junkers* is an old man's reminiscence of vanished youth, glimpsed through the mists of time and surrounded with an aura of alluring charm. Through Alexandrov, his younger self, Kuprin looks fondly back on his years in the Military Academy in Moscow as an ideal time, when love was novel and life just beginning. "Father wanted to forget himself," writes Kuprin's daughter Kseniya, "he wanted to compose something like a fairytale."[5] As Soviet critics are quick to note, *The Junkers* lacks the sharply critical tone of "At the Turning Point" and *The Duel*. Instead, Alexandrov's years as a junker are an idyll in a delightful establishment whose staff are benevolently solicitous of their charges and never resort to the rod. Time had clothed the past in a rosy light for the author who had so often denounced violence. Yet for all its sentimentality, Kuprin's idealized picture of bygone days lends *The Junkers* an indubitable charm. With a sad lyricism tempered by the boisterous optimism of youth, he explores such signal moments in Alexandrov's life as the first stirrings of love and the blossoming of literary creativity. Kuprin did not conceal the fact that Alexandrov was his younger double, and in Part I devotes two chapters to his earliest writings and his first tale, "The Last Debut." In view of this, it is odd that elsewhere Kuprin attempts to distance himself from his hero, notably by having him become not a writer but a painter.

The Junkers is valuable in the documentary sense not only for the light it sheds on Kuprin's early years but also for the picture it provides of his milieu. Many of its secondary characters are real and appear under their real names, from Alexandrov's friends to officers and teachers at the Academy. No less interesting are the festive glimpses of Moscow at Shrovetide and Christmas in the 1890s, with the thrill of high speed troika rides through the snowy streets and the glittering magic of winter balls at the Ekaterinsky Institute for girls. Yet colorful as they are, such decorative scenes only emphasize Kuprin's nostalgia for the Moscow of his youth and heighten the sadly retrospective flavor of his lyrical memoir.

A more moving evocation of the life of an émigré is *Jeannette,* the last significant work of Kuprin's career. Begun in the early 1920s and set in Passy, it describes the affection felt by an elderly professor, Simonov, for a little girl in his neighborhood. Though Simonov's biography and character differ from Kuprin's, his sadness and loneliness are clearly the author's own. Moreover, his memories of bygone years and the numerous reflective digressions in the tale contain many echoes of Kuprin's own past. In his tomb-like garret or on his lonely walks in the Bois de Boulogne, Simonov recalls his unhappy past, with its hasty marriage, divorce, and the daughters he never saw grow up. When into the sadness of his life little Jeannette bursts like a gay tornado, she releases all his pent-up affection. This impish creature, with her grubby face and hair as black as a Japanese doll's, transforms his life. But his happiness is cruelly brief, for the girl's mother leaves Paris and he loses Jeannette forever. Now his solitude is more painful still as, surrounded by the fog of a Parisian evening, he sits in his dark room with only his cat for company. Imbued with the sadness of solitary old age and with regret for the irrevocable past, *Jeannette* is a moving distillation of Kuprin's own feelings in the last years of his emigration.

The 1930s brought increasing hardship to Kuprin and his family. The difficulties caused by poverty were intensified by his sinking morale and declining health. The long separation from Russia was taking its toll, as he had confessed to the artist Ilya Repin in 1924: "Émigré life has completely chewed me up, while remoteness from my homeland has flattened my spirit to the ground."[6] Always preferring to portray life as he himself had lived it, he found it increasingly difficult to write about Russia from a distance and from memory. "The cocoon of my imagination has unwound," he wrote sadly in 1924, "and there are only five or six turns of silk thread left in it!"[7] His despair at his failing creativity led to the heavy drinking that dogged his Parisian years.[8] After 1932 his sight began to deteriorate, and his handwriting became so impaired that after *Jeannette* he wrote only four short tales.

Kuprin's longing for Russia grew more acute with every passing year. "It's the duty of every true patriot to return there," he wrote, "and it . . . would be sweeter and easier to die there."[9] When visas were granted early in 1937, Kuprin and his wife arranged to go first, leaving their daughter to follow (in the event she did not do so until 1958).[10] Thrilled at the prospect of returning to his beloved Russia, Kuprin believed he stood on the threshold of a new life.

CHAPTER 8

Epilogue

T HOUGH bewildered by the immense changes he found in Moscow, Kuprin resolved to assimilate his countless new impressions and make his contribution to Soviet life. But the long years in Paris had broken his health and transformed him into an old man. The tragic change was noticed by the writer Nikolay Teleshov, his friend of the early 1900s. Visiting him shortly after his arrival, Teleshov found him confused, rambling, and pathetic. "He left Russia . . . physically very robust and strong," he wrote later, "but returned an emaciated, . . . feeble, weak-willed invalid. This was no longer Kuprin — that man of outstanding talent — it was something . . . weak, sad, and visibly dying."[1]

Such was Kuprin's debility that he wrote practically nothing after his return to Russia. The two short pieces he did produce appeared in newspapers in 1937. To mark the first anniversary of Gorky's death in June, *Izvestiya* published Kuprin's "Otryvki vospominanii" ("Fragments of Memoirs"), which described his meetings with Gorky and paid homage to him as a writer.[2] October saw the publication of the sketch "Moskva rodnaia" ("My Native Moscow"), the result of an interview given to the paper *Komsomol'skaia pravda* (*Komsomol Truth,* organ of the communist youth organization), in which Kuprin expressed his joy at returning to Moscow and his gratitude for the welcome he had received.[3]

However, it seems he was not as euphoric about his return as his official interviews assert. In her revealing account of Kuprin's last months, Lidia Nord paints a picture of a disillusioned old man who felt he was a stranger in his native country.[4] Indignant at the censor's removal of *The Pit* from a proposed edition of his works, Kuprin criticized Soviet notions of morality. Objecting to pressure

153

put on him to write on contemporary Soviet subjects, he said: "Collective farm themes are not for me: I never wrote about the peasants before and I hardly know them.... There's no music to me in the sound of machines.... I know very little about the life of workers.... These themes have never interested me."[5] But even worse than this was the knowledge that he was being watched — something he had feared before he left France. Embittered by the authorities' apparent mistrust of him, he concluded that all the fine things said to him in Paris about his being necessary to Russia were only empty words.

January of 1938 brought a deterioration in Kuprin's health, and he realized that he would never write the great work of which he had dreamed on his return. By early July his condition was grave, and death was only a question of time. Though sadly it had stimulated no new creativity, his return to the USSR had fulfilled the dream of his long years in emigration. "One should die in Russia, at home," he once told a Parisian journalist, "just like a wild animal in the forest that goes off to its lair to die."[6]

*   *   *   *

Kuprin's position in the history of Russian literature is highly significant, if not unique. Born into an age overshadowed by the great Russian novel, which had reached its zenith in the 1860s, he turned to the short story as the genre suited both to his own restless temperament and to the manifold preoccupations of his generation. In both war and peace that generation was to witness social and political upheaval on a scale unprecedented even in Russia's tortured history, and in his writing Kuprin would reflect the turmoil of his time. With his contemporaries Chekhov, Gorky, and Bunin, he brought the genre of the short story to an efflorescence without parallel in Russian letters. What he conceded in restraint to Chekhov, conviction to Gorky, and subtlety to Bunin, Kuprin made up for in narrative pace, construction of plot, and richness of theme. These latter qualities, coupled with his abiding interest in the human soul, make him still very readable today.

As this study has shown, Kuprin was a writer of lived experience par excellence, and it is his constant focus on the details of actuality that lends his work its convincing power. His lifelong conviction that art should be fused indissolubly with reality explains the irritation and even hostility he felt toward contemporaries who ignored or denied that fusion. His strong dislike of the Symbolists and Decadents around the turn of the century illustrates the point.

While Gorky's *Knowledge* of which Kuprin was a member, became the center of progressive literary activity of a realistic kind, an opposite camp was formed by Symbolist and Decadent writers. Konstantin Balmont, Valery Bryusov, Dmitry Merezhkovsky, and others were primarily writers for the few: they resented the great success of *Knowledge* with the reading public and attacked what they considered vulgar, outmoded realism. Kuprin made no secret of the fact that he had nothing in common with such "high priests of the celebrated 'new beauty' " (IX, 79), as he called them, and was contemptuous of their work because it bore so little relation to actuality. For the same reason his opinion of much of Leonid Andreev's work, with its complex metaphysical abstractions, was generally unfavorable. And yet, despite his affinity for both the *Wednesday* and *Knowledge* circles, Kuprin was never truly *of* them. His was too vigorously dynamic, too fiercely independent a spirit to suffer for long the constraints inevitably imposed on the individualist by a coterie whose growing tendentiousness was epitomized by Gorky. Thus Kuprin cannot correctly be viewed as belonging totally to any literary grouping of his time. Instead, he might best be described simply as one of the most distinguished Russian realistic prose writers of the early 1900s. As in his immensely varied life, so in his writing, he traveled his own road.

Kuprin's talent is essentially optimistic, assertive of life in all its manifestations. Despite the gloom of his declining years, his career was devoted to the exaltation of man and the beauty of natural things. Perhaps the most eloquent summary of his art may be found in his own words on the death of Tolstoy in 1910, for they apply equally well to himself: "He showed us, who are dull and blind, the beauty of the earth, the sky, men and animals. He told us, who are mean and distrustful, that everyone can be good, compassionate, attractive, and beautiful at heart" (IX, 122–23). As generous and all-embracing as the life it extols, Kuprin's giant spirit strides the pages of his works with a vigor time cannot diminish.

Notes and References

Chapter One

1. Ivan Bunin, *Memories and Portraits* (London, 1951), p. 90.
2. *Ibid.*, p. 91.
3. F.I. Kuleshov, ed., *A.I. Kuprin o literature* (Minsk, 1969), p. 24. Hereinafter cited as *Kuprin o literature*.
4. F.I. Kuleshov, *Tvorcheskii put' Kuprina* (Minsk, 1963), p. 19.
5. Her first two sons, Innokenty and Boris, had died in infancy.
6. P.N. Berkov, *Aleksandr Ivanovich Kuprin* (Moscow-Leningrad, 1956), p. 6.
7. V.N. Afanas'ev, *Aleksandr Ivanovich Kuprin* (Moscow, 1960), p. 6.
8. During these years Kuprin also made several translations of foreign verse, among them Béranger's *Les Hirondelles* (1885), Heine's *Lorelei* (1887) and Kerner's *Der reichste Fürst* (1887). He went on translating for most of his career.
9. F.I. Kuleshov, "Iz neizdannykh stikhotvorenii A.I. Kuprina," *Uchenye zapiski,* Tom II, *Stat'i o literature,* Iuzhnosakhalinskii gosud. ped. instit. (Sakhalin, 1959), p. 180.
10. *Ibid.*, p. 183.
11. Kuleshov, *Tvorcheskii put' Kuprina*, p. 94.
12. *Ibid.*, p. 95.
13. *Ibid.*, p. 85.
14. In Alarin's inclination for introspection Kuleshov detects psychological affinities with the "superfluous men" of Pushkin, Lermontov and Turgenev, as well as with later Kuprinian heroes like Bobrov (*Moloch*) and Romashov (*The Duel*). See *Ibid.*, p. 86.
15. See A. Volkov, *Tvorchestvo A.I. Kuprina* (Moscow, 1962), p. 17.
16. See note, I, 490.
17. See *Moskva,* 3 (1958), 118–19.

Chapter Two

1. Berkov, p. 16.
2. Kuleshov, p. 61.

3. For pseudonyms see I.F. Masanov, *Slovar' psevdonimov,* Moscow, 1956–60, Vol. 4, p. 264.

4. See P.P. Shirmakov, "Neizvestnaia p'esa A.I. Kuprina *Gran' stoletiia,*" *Leningradskii al'manakh,* 11 (1956), 373–82.

5. See IX, 69–71.

6. Kuleshov, p. 76.

7. For examples of sketches see Berkov, p. 18.

8. A. Kuprin, *Kievskie tipy* (Kiev, 1896), p. 3.

9. See II, 496.

10. See, for example, Kuleshov, pp. 120–22.

11. Afanas'ev, p. 17.

12. Kuleshov, p. 126.

13. Berkov, p. 25.

14. Volkov, p. 48.

15. Berkov, p. 32.

16. *Kuprin o literature,* p. 196.

17. The same device of a sympathetic interlocutor designed to draw from his partner what the author needs was to appear again in *The Duel* (Nazansky) and *The Pit* (Platonov).

18. *Moloch, Russkoe bogatstvo,* 12 (1896), 125. All but Bobrov's first sentence was cut from later versions.

19. *Kuprin o literature,* p. 196. For details of the work's composition and revision see I.A. Pitliar, *"Moloch," Uchenye zapiski* Leningradskogo gosud. ped. instit., 43 (1947), 134–54.

20. Berkov, p. 31.

21. *The Oxford Chekhov,* vol. IX (1975), p. 74.

22. Berkov, p. 33.

23. This period is reflected in Kuprin's tale "Zapechatannye mladentsy" ("The Buried Infants") (1915), in which he lists some of his temporary occupations (see VII, 14).

24. Kuleshov, p. 161.

25. See note, II, 500.

26. Afanas'ev p. 43.

27. B.M. Kiselev, *Rasskazy o Kuprine* (Moscow, 1964), p. 175.

28. V.V. Vorovskii, "A.I. Kuprin," in *Literaturno-kriticheskie stat'i* (Moscow, 1956), p. 275.

29. See note, II, 504.

Chapter Three

1. See I.V. Koretskaia, "Chekhov i Kuprin," in *Literaturnoe nasledstvo,* vol. 68 (Moscow, 1960), pp. 363–94; and F.D. Batiushkov, "Chekhov i Kuprin," *Severnie zori,* No. 1, (December 11, 1909), cols. 19–25.

2. See L. Nikulin, "Kuprin i Bunin," *Oktiabr',* 7 (1958), 204–18; and Bunin.

3. See E.M. Aspiz, "S A.I. Kuprinym v Danilovskom," *Literaturnaia Vologda,* 5 (1959), 180–91.

4. See *Kuprin o literature,* pp. 224–37; and I. Gura, "Pis'ma A.I. Kuprina k F.D. Batiushkovu iz Danilovskogo," in Almanac *Sever* (Vologda, 1963), pp. 152–58.

5. For letters of Kuprin to Miroliubov see P.P. Shirmakov, ed., "A.I. Kuprin. Pis'ma k V.S. Miroliubovu, 1899–1907," *Literaturnyi arkhiv,* vol. 5, ANSSSR (Moscow-Leningrad, 1960), pp. 118–27.

6. See I.V. Koretskaia, "Gor'kii i Kuprin," in *Gor'kovskie chteniia 1964–1965* (Moscow, 1966), pp. 119–61.

7. M.K. Kuprina-Iordanskaia, "Iz vospominanii o D.N. Mamine-Sibiriake," *D.N. Mamin-Sibiriak* (Sverdlovsk, 1953), p. 177.

8. *Kuprin o literature,* p. 208.

9. See Kuleshov, p. 198.

10. A. Bogdanovich, "Kriticheskie zametki," Mir bozhii, 4 (1903), 7–11.

11. See Afanas'ev, p. 51.

12. Volkov, p. 116.

13. See note, III, 472.

14. Afanas'ev, pp. 52–3.

15. *Kuprin o literature,* p. 197.

16. See Kuleshov, p. 187.

17. N. Asheshov, "Rasskazy A. Kuprina," *Vestnik i biblioteka samoobrazovaniia,* 17 (1903), p. 747.

18. Volkov, p. 133.

19. See his article on Kuprin in *Vestnik literatury,* 8 (1905), pp. 161–68.

Chapter Four

1. Kuleshov, p. 207.

2. M.K. Kuprina-Iordanskaia, *Gody molodosti* (Moscow, 1966), p. 121.

3. *Ibid.,* p. 81. Though it is technically a tale (*povest'*), Kuprin often called *The Duel* a novel (*roman*). In 1937, for example, he wrote: "...the *Knowledge* publishing house published my first big tale or rather novel — *The Duel*" (see IX, 66).

4. *Ibid.,* pp. 130–31.

5. Volkov, p. 168.

6. Kuprin describes the episode in "Moi pasport" ("My Passport") of 1908 (V, 119–23).

7. Volkov, p. 165.

8. *Kuprin o literature,* p. 221.

9. Afanas'ev, p. 69. The dedication was dropped in later editions.

10. Kuleshov, p. 280.

11. Though many saw *The Duel* as the artistic spearhead of that attack, it would be wrong to overemphasize its connections with 1905 or the

Russo-Japanese War in the way many Soviet commentators do. It was after all begun over a decade before, and had its writing gone more smoothly, would have been published well before 1905. Its appearance at a time of crisis owed more to chance than good management.

12. Kuleshov, p. 258.

13. See *ibid.*, p. 251.

14. When it does finally emerge, Romashov's biography parallels Kuprin's own: Romashov is from Narovchat in Penza Province; has only a mother, having lost his father at an early age; was educated in boarding school, Cadet Corps and Military Academy. He is making his first attempts at literary work, and the title of his third tale is *The Last Fatal Debut.*

15. Volkov, p. 189.

16. *K.N. Batiushkov, F.D. Batiushkov, A.I. Kuprin* (Vologda, 1968), p. 129.

17. *Ibid.*, p. 133. Nazansky might even be seen as Romashov's double, representing the broken officer Romashov may well have become had he not been killed and had remained in the army.

18. Kuleshov, p. 240.

19. To a lesser extent, the link manifests itself in Romashov too, who is ashamed of his bespectacled plainness. After his first spell of thoughtfulness while under house arrest, Shurochka tells him he has "even grown more handsome" (IV, 66).

20. Gareth Williams, "Romashov and Nazansky: Enemies of the People," *Canadian Slavonic Papers,* IX, no. 2 (1967), 194-200. For an examination of Stirner's work see J. Carroll, *Break-Out from the Crystal Palace, the anarchopsychological critique: Stirner, Nietzsche, Dostoevsky* (London, 1974).

21. Max Stirner, *The Ego and his Own,* tr. S. Byington (New York, 1918), p. 309.

22. *Ibid.*, p. 171.

23. *Ibid.*, p. 178.

24. *Ibid.*, p. 174.

25. *Ibid.*, pp. 197-98.

26. *Ibid.*, p. 268.

27. *Ibid.*, p. 187.

28. *Ibid.*, p. 338.

29. *Ibid.*, p. 190.

30. *Ibid.*, p. 387.

31. *Ibid.*, p. 386.

32. Williams, p. 196.

33. Stirner, p. 381.

34. Kuleshov, p. 268.

35. *Ibid.*

36. L.V. Krutikova, *A.I. Kuprin* (Leningrad, 1971), pp. 55-56.

37. Berkov, p. 56.
38. Kuleshov, p. 273.
39. *Ibid.*, p. 260.
40. *Ibid.*, p. 278.
41. Afanas'ev, pp. 88–89.
42. Afanas'ev, p. 70.
43. *Ibid.*, p. 69.
44. *Ibid.*, p. 71.
45. See *K.N. Batiushkov, F.D. Batiushkov, A.I. Kuprin, op. cit.,* p. 131.
46. See *Peterburgskie vedomosti,* No. 149 (June 21, 1905), p. 2.
47. See Berkov, *op. cit.,* p. 61.
48. Drozd-Boniachevskii, *"Poedinok" Kuprina s tochki zreniia stroevogo ofitsera,* St. Petersburg, 1910.
49. Alexander Kuprin, "Armee und Revolution in Russland," *Neue freie Presse* (Vienna), 15103 (September 8, 1906), 2–3.
50. Perhaps unconsciously, Kuprin was less than honest here. See the articles by V. Afanas'ev ("Sovremennitsa *Poedinka," Ogonek,* 36 (1960), 19; and "Na podstupakh k *Poedinku," Russkaia literatura,* 4 (1961), 159–63), which show that many characters in *The Duel* are based on actual people.
51. For an account of Kuprin's difficulties with his last chapter see T. Osharova, "Kuprin v rabote nad finalom *Poedinka," Russkaia literatura,* 3 (1966), 179–85.
52. Volkov, p. 203.
53. Kuprina-Iordanskaia, *Gody molodosti,* p. 231. In his sequel Kuprin intended to have Romashov meet Shurochka as a prostitute in Kiev. During her final meeting with Romashov she said that if her husband failed to enter the Academy she would leave him and seek her fortune in Petersburg, Odessa, or Kiev: "I'll do violence to myself, but I'll burn myself out in a single instant as brilliantly as a firework!" (IV, 215). For further details of *The Beggars,* see Kuleshov, pp. 415–20.
54. See Kuleshov, p. 416.

Chapter Five

1. For an account of Kuprin's part in the rescue, see E.M. Aspiz, "A.I. Kuprin v Balaklave," *Krym,* 23 (1959), 131–36.
2. Vorovskii, p. 278.
3. Sashka's real name was Gol'dshtein, and Paustovsky recalls how he was buried with pomp in starving Odessa in 1921. See K. Paustovsky, "Potok zhizni" (Zametki o proze Kuprina), in *Sobranie sochinenii v shesti tomakh,* Moscow, 1958, vol. 5, pp. 629–55.
4. Kuleshov, p. 349.
5. Volkov, p. 207.

6. See note, V, 487–88.
7. See IV, 398.
8. See IX, 72–75.
9. A relative of the Siberian writer Mamin-Sibiriak, Elizaveta Geinrikh had lived as a child with Alexandra Davydova, editor of *God's World,* and thus knew Kuprin's first wife. During the war with Japan she had served as a nurse.
10. Kuprina-Iordanskaia, *Gody molodosti,* p. 243.
11. Kuleshov, p. 382.
12. Afanas'ev, p. 109.
13. Temira Pachmuss, *Zinaida Hippius. An Intellectual Profile* (Carbondale, Illinois, 1971), p. 340. Kuprin's own opinion of *Sulamith* was unfavorable: "It's an artificial thing ... a collection of bookish information, excerpts and quotations ... very skillfully written but cold." (Krutikova, p. 83.)
14. See L. Liubimov, "Na chuzhbine," *Novyi mir,* 2 (1957), 181–87; and "Iz tvorcheskoi laboratorii Kuprina," *Russkaia literatura,* 4 (1961), 164–67.
15. Letter of December 3, 1910, from Odessa, in *Kuprin o literature,* p. 237.
16. Volkov, p. 353.
17. Krutikova, p. 86.
18. A. Izmailov, "Pod krasnym fonarem," *Russkoe slovo,* 91 (April 22, 1909) 2. For other views of *Yama* see, for example: Vl. Kranikhfel'd, "Literaturnye otkliki," *Sovremennyi mir,* 6 (1909), 98–102; K. Chukovskii, "Novaia kniga A.I. Kuprina," *Niva,* 45 (November 8, 1914), 867–70; V.G. Golikov, "*Yama* Kuprina," *Vestnik znaniia,* 6 (1915), 360–69.
19. See Kuleshov, p. 423.
20. *Ibid.,* p. 424.
21. Afanas'ev, p. 136.
22. Kuleshov, p. 428.
23. Berkov, p. 134.

Chapter Six

1. Letter to Batiushkov of October 8. 1910, from Odessa, in *Kuprin o literature,* p. 235.
2. Volkov, p. 318.
3. Kuleshov, p. 431.
4. *Ibid.,* p. 432.
5. *Ibid.,* p. 438. For the text of Gorky's letter see Berkov, pp. 100-101.
6. Kuleshov, p. 456.
7. Afanas'ev, p. 150.
8. Kuleshov, p. 478.
9. Afanas'ev, p. 156.

10. The episode is described in Kuprin's tale "Shestoe chuvstvo" ("Sixth Sense"), in *Zhaneta* (Paris, 1934), pp. 75-108. The work contains unflattering references to the Bolsheviks and criticizes them for causing a revolution in wartime, calling it "a crime before the homeland" (p. 100).

11. See A.I. Kuprin, *Elan': Rasskazy* (Belgrade, 1929), pp. 125-32.

12. For details of *Land* and Kuprin's meeting with Lenin, see Kuleshov, pp. 482-84.

13. For an account of and excerpts from both, see P. Shirmakov, "Novye stranitsy rukopisei," *Neva,* 9 (1970), pp. 181-89.

14. In his sketch "Nemnozhko Finlandii" ("A Little of Finland," 1908), Kuprin wrote: "Politics are completely alien to me, and I would never wish to play the role of a forecaster or organizer of the destinies of peoples" (V, 64).

15. *Kuprin o literature,* p. 20.

Chapter Seven

1. See IX, 156–58.

2. *Kuprin o literature,* p. 246.

3. Letter to Ivan Zaikin of spring 1924, *ibid.*, p. 258.

4. Kuleshov, p. 503.

5. Krutikova, pp. 112–13.

6. K.A. Kuprina, *Kuprin — moi otets* (Moscow, 1971), p. 173.

7. Kuprina-Iordanskaia, *Gody molodosti,* p. 323.

8. See V. Unkovsky, "O Kuprine," *Grani* (Frankfurt), 21, pp. 79-82. A much more attractive picture of the aging Kuprin is painted by L. Arsen'eva, ("O Kuprine," *Grani,* 43, pp. 125-32), who disagrees with Unkovsky's account.

9. Kuprina-Iordanskaia, *Gody molodosti,* p. 323.

10. Though Kuprin's wife and daughter certainly encouraged him to return and made arrangements for the journey, Bunin was guilty of exaggeration in asserting that Kuprin's role was purely passive: "He did not go to Russia — he was taken there, very ill, already in his second childhood" (Bunin, pp. 96–97). Similarly, Unkovsky maintains that Kuprin knew nothing about his return to the USSR and did not understand what was happening when he left Paris.

Chapter Eight

1. N. Teleshov, *Zapiski pisatelia* (Moscow, 1943), p. 87.

2. See IX, 65–66.

3. See VIII, 553–56.

4. Lidia Nord, "Vozvrashchenie A.I. Kuprina," *Inzhenery dush* (Buenos Aires, 1954), pp. 60–64.

5. *Ibid.,* p. 61

6. Kuprina, p. 234.

Selected Bibliography

PRIMARY SOURCES

Polnoe sobranie sochinenii v deviati tomakh, St. Petersburg-Petrograd, A.F. Marks, 1912–15.
Kupol' sv. Isaakiia Dalmatskogo, Riga, "Literatura," 1928.
Elan': rasskazy, Belgrade, 1929.
Zhaneta: roman, Paris, "Vozrozhdenie," 1934.
Sochineniia v trekh tomakh, Moscow, GIKhL, 1953.
Sobranie sochinenii v shesti tomakh, Moscow, Goslitizdat, 1957–58.
Sobranie sochinenii v deviati tomakh, Moscow, "Pravda," 1964.
Sobranie sochinenii v deviati tomakh, Moscow, "Khudozhestvennaia literatura," 1970–73.
Yama (The Pit), tr. B.G. Guerney, New York, Modern Library, 1932.
The Duel and Selected Stories, tr. A.R. MacAndrew, New York, New American Library, 1961.
Gambrinus and Other Stories, tr. B.G. Guerney, Freeport, Books for Libraries Press, 1970.
A Slav Soul and Other Stories, Freeport, Books for Libraries Press, 1971.

SECONDARY SOURCES

1. Books.

AFANAS'EV, VLADISLAV. *Aleksandr Ivanovich Kuprin, Kritiko-biograficheskii ocherk,* Moscow, GIKhL, 1960. The most useful short study of Kuprin's life and works.
BERKOV, PAVEL. *Aleksandr Ivanovich Kuprin, Kritiko-biograficheskii ocherk,* Moscow-Leningrad, ANSSSR, 1956. The earliest study of Kuprin. Several omissions and scant detail on later years, particularly emigration.
DYNNIK, ALEKSANDR. *A.I. Kuprin: ocherk zhizni i tvorchestva,* East Lansing, Michigan, Izd. Russian Language Journal, 1969. Superficial and unsatisfactory account. Many glaring omissions, inaccuracies, and blunders.
KRUTIKOVA, LIUDMILA. *A.I. Kuprin,* Leningrad, "Prosveshchenie," 1971. Brief but well-written and useful study of general kind.

KULESHOV, FEDOR. *Tvorcheskii put' A.I. Kuprina,* Minsk, MVSSO, 1963. Lengthy and very detailed biographical and critical study, researched with scrupulous care. Easily the best work on Kuprin to date.

KULESHOV, FEDOR, ed. *A.I. Kuprin o literature,* Minsk, Izd-vo BGU, 1969. Comprehensive selection of Kuprin's letters, critical articles, and some lesser known tales.

KUPRINA, KSENIIA. *Kuprin — moi otets,* Moscow, "Sovetskaia Rossiia," 1971. Biographical account with much interesting detail on years of Kuprin's emigration.

KUPRINA-IORDANSKAIA, MARIIA. *Gody molodosti,* Moscow, "Khudozhestvennaia literatura," 1966. Biographical account. Especially informative on early years of Kuprin's career and writing of *The Duel.*

VERZHBITSKII, NIKOLAI. *Vstrechi s A.I. Kuprinym,* Penza, Penzenskoe kn. izd-vo, 1961. Personal reminiscences of Kuprin. Anecdotal but amusing and intriguing.

VOLKOV, ANATOLII. *Tvorchestvo A.I. Kuprina,* Moscow, "Sovetskii pisatel'," 1962. Long critical study. Instructive but annoyingly vague and diffuse in places.

2. Essays and articles

ADAMOVICH, GEORGII. "Kuprin," *Odinochestvo i svoboda,* New York, 1955, pp. 243-49. Brief but useful general remarks on Kuprin's major works.

BRUSIANIN, VASILII. "Deti v proizvedeniiakh A.I. Kuprina," *Deti i pisateli,* Moscow, 1915, pp. 204-72. Study of Kuprin's portrayal of children and animals.

CHUKOVSKII, KORNEI. "Kuprin," *Novyi mir,* No. 3, 1962, pp. 190-210. General article of a biographical kind.

GURA, I. "Povest' A.I. Kuprina *Poedinok,*" *Voprosy zhanra i stilia,* pod. red. V.V. Gura, Vologda, 1967, pp. 84-116. Useful essay on *The Duel,* with examination of language, style and changes made in early drafts.

IZMAILOV, ALEKSANDR. "Pesni zemnoi radosti," *Literaturnyi Olimp,* Moscow, 1911, pp. 339-69. Sensitive and wide-ranging article, stressing Kuprin's indomitable love of life.

JACKSON, ROBERT. "A.I. Kuprin's *River of Life,*" *Dostoevsky's Underground Man in Russian Literature,* The Hague, 1958, pp. 108-112. Interesting essay drawing parallels between hero of Kuprin's tale and the Underground Man.

KORETSKAIA, I.V. "A.I. Kuprin," *Sochineniia v trekh tomakh,* Moscow, 1953, pp. III-XXXIX. Very useful general article on Kuprin's biography and works.

KRANIKHFEL'D, VLADIMIR. "Poet radostnoi sluchainosti," *Sovremennyi mir,* No. 4, 1908, pp. 52-79. Perceptive survey of Kuprin's earlier work.

KULESHOV, FEDOR. "Aleksandr Ivanovich Kuprin," in A.I. Kuprin, *Sobranie sochinenii v deviati tomakh,* Moscow, 1970, I, 5-38. Excellent biographical and critical essay.

MIKHAILOVSKII, BORIS. "Tvorchestvo A.I. Kuprina," *Russkaia literatura XX veka,* Moscow, 1939, pp. 47-58. Informative survey which unfortunately dismisses Kuprin's work in emigration in a single sentence.

NIKULIN, LEV. *Chekhov. Bunin. Kuprin,* Moscow, 1960, pp. 267-325. General account, mainly biographical in content.

PLOTKIN, LEV. "A.I. Kuprin," *Literaturnye ocherki i stat'i,* Leningrad, 1958, pp. 413-45. Detailed survey article, especially good on Kuprin's earlier work.

SEDYKH, ANDREI. "A.I. Kuprin," *Dalekie, blizkie,* New York, 1962, pp. 7-17. Chiefly biographical account of Kuprin's years in Paris.

SHIRMAKOV, P.P. "Novoe ob A.I. Kuprine," *Russkaia literatura,* No. 2, 1962, pp. 205-12. Material on Kuprin's biography in early 1900's, with his letters to L.I. Elpat'evskaia.

SOBOLEV, YURII. "A.I. Kuprin," *Obshchestudencheskii literaturnyi sbornik,* Moscow, 1910, pp. 137-78. One of the earliest general essays on Kuprin, examining themes, moods, and characterizations in some depth.

STRUVE, GLEB. *Russkaia literatura v izgnanii,* New York, 1956, pp. 99-101, 267-68. Interesting details on Kuprin's editorship of White Army newspaper, his work as a journalist in Finland, and his years in Paris.

VISHNEVSKY, IVAN. "A.I. Kuprin," *Povesti i rasskazy,* Lvov, 1958, pp. 3-17. Readable survey article, though includes nothing on Kuprin's work in emigration.

VOLKOV, ANATOLII. "A.I. Kuprin," *Russkaia literatura XX veka,* Moscow, 1966, pp. 277-303. Useful general account, both biographical and critical.

WILLIAMS, GARETH. "Romashov and Nazansky: Enemies of the People," *Canadian Slavonic Papers,* Vol. IX, No. 2 (1967), pp. 194-200. Interesting discussion of the link between the philosophy of Max Stirner and two major characters in *The Duel.*

Index

(The works of Kuprin are listed under his name)